LEADING WITH NLP

ESSENTIAL LEADERSHIP SKILLS FOR
INFLUENCING AND MANAGING PEOPLE

Joseph O'Connor

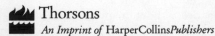
Thorsons
An Imprint of HarperCollins*Publishers*

Thorsons
An Imprint of HarperCollins*Publishers*
77–85 Fulham Palace Road
Hammersmith, London W6 8JB

Published by Thorsons 1998

10 9 8 7 6 5 4 3 2 1

A catalogue record for this book
is available from the British Library

ISBN 0 7225 3767 0

Printed and bound in Great Britain by
Creative Print & Design, (Ebbw Vale) Wales

CONTENTS

INTRODUCTION:
THE LEADER'S JOURNEY

Two people died in the same week in August 1997, Princess
Diana in Paris and Mother Teresa in Calcutta. They could
hardly have been more different on the surface. Princess
Diana was rich, famous, beautiful and controversial. Mother
Teresa was an elderly Albanian nun who slept on a hard bed
and worked with the poor and sick on the streets of Calcutta.
Yet both touched people's hearts; they were loved and respected as well as being international figures. They were
leaders. When they died, people who had never met them
mourned them. Why?

Because both were not perfect icons but real people with
human frailties that others could identify with. They were
like us, yet they expressed something of the best in us –
something of what we are and *could* be. These two people
were in the public eye, like many others we regard as leaders
– politicians, artists, musicians and businessmen – but leadership is more than a job description. Leadership is a way of
acting and a way of being that we all can have, not something
'out there', something for other, famous people. At *every*
level leaders have the ability to help people, express their
hopes and carry their fears. I would like this book to demys-
tify leadership, taking it down from its high pedestal and
making it a natural part of life.

In the past, leaders were the rich, the powerful and the
famous, great kings, warlords, scientists and thinkers, outstanding artists or craftsmen, or giants of commerce.
Literature and history hold them up as examples and it
seems we can only aspire to be pale copies. Over the twenti-
eth century there has been a profound democratization in

almost every aspect of human life, except leadership. At first sight this seems to make sense – after all, we can't *all* be leaders, can we? No. Not if we continue to accept a narrow definition of leadership based on power, high profile and wide authority.

Let us reclaim leadership to its original meaning: taking a path or going on a journey. Leadership is the journey itself, the activity, not the destination – a stimulating and fulfilling journey where planning and preparation are also important and enjoyable in their own right.

I see leadership skills as the most important resource we have to develop to deal with the capricious times in which we live. That we live in times of rapid change is a truism – we have to adapt to the sort of breakneck changes in one life-time that previously would have taken generations. In the world of business, markets and strategies change fast. We are on a high-technology carousel that never seems to slow down. The carousel spins with bewildering speed as we strive to deal with the present and shape the future but with systems and organizations designed to cope with the past. We have more information, but knowledge – information that matters and makes a difference – is as hard as ever to acquire. We take a sieve to the torrent of information that drenches us every day and hope to catch something of value.

How can we pin down leadership, one of the most talked about and written about subjects in business? Is it charisma? Influence? Inspiration? Stewardship? Yes. It may be. Because the reason you set out on your journey, your chosen destination, who you travel with and how you travel may all vary. That's what is so infuriating and valuable about leadership. There are many roads, many destinations and many ways to travel.

So why learn to be a leader? To be involved in what really matters to you. To be able to do what inspires and moves you. To have companions on your journey. In any area where you want more influence you must be a leader.

Leadership has a paradox at its centre – while greatly prized, you cannot grab it for yourself directly. It is a gift which can only be given by others. Being a leader has no meaning without others who choose to travel with you. A leader all alone is like the sound of one hand clapping.

So this book represents a journey in three senses. First it has travellers' tales from leaders on their path. What was it like for them? What did they find? Where are the pitfalls and the dragons on the path? What essential travel equipment do we need? These tales come from all over the world. Secondly, this book is a practical tour guide for you to prepare in your imagination what you want to do in reality. Thirdly, this book is itself a journey. I have a plan and a vision of what it will be about and what it will do. I have my map, but the writing has a momentum and direction of its own and right now I do not know exactly what route we will take. I know where we need to arrive, but there are many fascinating sights to see, sounds to hear and places to explore on the way. We do not know what exactly we shall find in them and there may be some unscheduled stops on the way.

This is a personal view of leadership. For me, three areas of leadership stand out: self-development, influencing and communication skills, and systemic thinking.

First, being a leader means developing yourself. You need to be strong and resourceful in order to make the journey. As you become a leader, you find resources in yourself you did not know you had. You become more yourself, because a leader's greatest influence comes from who they are, what they do and the example they set. Secondly, a leader inspires others to join them on the road, so leadership involves communication and influencing skills. Otherwise you are a lone traveller, not a leader. Thirdly, a leader must look towards their destination, as well as paying attention to where they have been and where they are. Without such a road map, however strong they may be and however many companions they may have, they may get lost down a cul-de-sac or stuck in a swamp. A leader needs to understand the system they are part of, to see beyond the obvious, beyond the immediate situation, to sense how events connect to deeper patterns. So leadership is a combination of who you are, the skills and talents you have, and your understanding of the situation or the context you are in. While these elements are universal, you will put the pieces together in a way unique to you.

You can use this book in any area of your life where you want the benefits of being a leader. I will concentrate, however, on business examples because leadership is so important in business and business holds so many opportunities to be a leader.

Leadership is no easy 'faddish' package that you can hand out as part of a corporate restructure to solve all your problems. It needs work; you need to develop the ability to respond to challenge as well as deal with the specific challenges that arise in the course of your business. I want to look at leadership from the inside as well as the outside. What are the most useful ways to think about managing a business? What skills are needed? Leadership holds some answers to these questions.

The Management Agenda, a report published by the Roffey Park Management Institute in 1998, contained the replies of a sample of managers to questions on work issues. Many were critical of senior managers for lacking leadership. At the same time, they said that they themselves were expected to be leaders, yet they had no training on what this involved or how to adjust to this new identity. There seems to be a need for leadership in business and at the same time a vacuum about what this means in practice and how to make the change.

Leadership is part of, and the result of, the great changes in management practice in the last 20 years. It replaces the old 'command and control' model of running an organization. 'Command and control', based on a military mentality, was appropriate in a different social climate and a stable business environment. Now this stability has gone, a casualty of a frenetic pace of change, new values of self-esteem and individual responsibility and a business culture that values employability above employment. In most business organizations, particularly in the Western world, we just do not obey orders any more – at least not without good reason. But leaders are still needed, both to guide the organization and to develop others as leaders.

Leadership is not a quality that can be rationed or controlled; rather, it is based on purpose, vision and values: *purpose* to set the destination, *vision* to see where you are going and *values* to guide you on the way towards a successful and sustainable future.

When I think of how organizational leadership could be, I think of the flight of a flock of birds. I watched a flock of starlings swoop over the horse chestnut trees close to where I live a few days ago. The birds moved together in beautiful and intricate patterns, moving away and then sweeping back, describing a sort of figure of eight, but no pass was quite like any other. How did they do it? There were one or more birds at the front, but they were not issuing orders to the others, telling them exactly how to move so they all stayed together. The leader (if the one at the front was the leader) was different every time they passed over my head. Yet somehow they not only flew together, but also kept in formation. They could adjust in a split second to keep the pattern, but the pattern was never identical from moment to moment. How did they stay together in that marvellous formation like liquid rolling through the air? How do starlings organize themselves, keeping their individuality and yet being part of a wider coherent group? There seems to be an intelligence that emerges from the group, coming from the intelligence of each member, yet larger than that possessed by any individual.

Leaders face the organizational challenge of creating the context where that larger intelligence can emerge without diminishing the individuals in any way. The more the individuals use their own intelligence to the full for themselves, the smarter the group becomes. This is the puzzle and the challenge of how individual and organizational learning work together. So, here is the secret of organizational leadership. How do you develop each person as a leader and get them all to fly in formation?

What resources do we have to help us achieve this? Neuro-Linguistic Programming (NLP) is a broad field that began in the mid-1970s modelling excellent communicators – finding out how they did what they did so well. NLP models how we do what we do. In essence it studies the structure of subjective experience – how we create our own unique internal world from what we see, hear and feel, and how in turn our mental world shapes what we allow ourselves to see, hear and feel. NLP has modelled top people in every field – managers, salespeople, teachers and trainers – in order to teach others these skills, so they do not have to reinvent the wheel. It has a wealth of material from leaders – how they think and what they believe.

NLP is made up of three parts:

- 'Neuro' is our neurology – how we think and feel.
- 'Linguistic' is the language part – what we say, how we say it and how we are influenced by what we hear.
- 'Programming' is how we act to achieve our results.

NLP helps us to understand what leaders do and how they get their results, so you can take those parts that suit you and that fit in with your values and beliefs. You don't *copy* them, you *learn from* them to achieve your goals. Whatever skills you have, NLP can help you make more of them. It also gives practical ways of developing those skills, not an intellectual appreciation of how nice the skills would be to have or how great they are in other people. NLP is a valuable guide on the leader's journey.

Our second guide on the journey is systemic thinking – thinking in terms of feedback and relationships, seeing patterns, not isolated events. Leaders have to understand the system they are in, and systems do not operate logically, small changes can produce large effects and these need not occur in the same place or at the same time as the cause. Straight-line cause and effect thinking does not work in business organizations, because they are complex systems. There may be many effects from just one change. Also, what you do to solve a problem may actually perpetuate it, or even make it worse in the long run. But when you think systemically, you think past the obvious to the dynamic patterns that generate a problem.

A third resource is the insights from the discipline of complexity science. Complexity is the application of systems thinking to complex systems (like business organizations) that behave in complicated ways. Recent research has given us some fascinating insights into complex systems that we can tentatively apply to business. For example, a few simple rules can generate very complex behaviour. What are the rules that hold the flock of birds together and how might those rules map over into creating a prosperous and successful organization? We can make some interesting speculations. Also, there seems to be an optimum point for a business – between the indolence of too much deadening procedure and the chaos of too much change. Too much order and the business becomes inflexible, too rigid to react quickly enough to the demands of the external market or the demands of the people within it. Too much freedom and the organization does not work either: rules change too quickly and people become disoriented and confused. People can learn best at the delicately poised point of balance between the two extremes. How can an organization get to this 'edge of chaos' with enough creativity to adapt to change, but within a structure stable enough to operate effectively? Getting to this edge is one of the main tasks of an organizational leader.

Finally, complex systems are not predictable. In theory they may be, but as the old saying goes, 'In theory there shouldn't be a difference between theory and practice, but in practice, there always is.' Complete control is impossible, and even if it were, it would be the kiss of death. There is no book, method or consultant that can tell you how to push the river (although many claim credit that it is their pushing that causes the river to move). But that does not mean you are helpless. Quite the opposite. It is a tremendous relief to admit that you cannot predict and therefore cannot entirely control a complex organization. You can give up trying. Now you can start to see how the organization really works and allow it to organize itself in the best way. This is a leader's work.

NLP explores how people think and the results they get. Complexity and systems thinking explore the organizations they create as they work together. These ideas are fascinating and practical – which is why I write about them. Together they are the basis of our map.

Organizations are fond of saying that the quality of the people who work in them gives them their competitive edge. At the risk of being heretical, I doubt this very much. Every organization has excellent people of high quality. The *leaders* make the difference. They determine the quality of the experience of working in that business, they weave that indefinable, yet very important fabric – the organizational culture. At the same time, I believe everyone in an organization can be a leader in some way. I hope this book is a step towards making this possible and real.

How to Use This Book

My goal in this book is to weave the three strands of leadership into a thread to guide you through the twists and turns of the leader's path. There are suggestions and exercises to develop yourself as a leader, to influence others in any situation where you are called on to lead, and to learn systemic thinking skills and apply them in a professional business context.

There are seven sections:

- The first begins the journey. It starts with your vision – why be a leader? What does it mean?
- The second section deals with different types of leaders and styles of leadership, explaining how when, where and why they are useful.
- The third section starts to move away from the present and looks at vision, values and purpose, both organizational and individual.

- The fourth looks at motivation and how to build it, also the dark side of leadership, the difficulties and obstacles.
- The fifth deals with resources on the journey — the maps, guides and rules of the road.
- The sixth looks at the guardians you will meet on the way and how to overcome them, how to build trust and be trust-worthy.
- The guardians are not only external difficulties such as resistance from other people and organizational inertia, but also your own internal resistances and blocks.
- The seventh section is about the skills and responsibilities you face as a leader and how you might get a business to fly in formation.
- The last section is about passing on the skills you have learned to others through coaching and mentoring. It also has a summary of the principles of leadership.
- There is also a resource section at the end with a bibliography.

Use this book to form your leadership skills, to develop yourself and others. Use it to stimulate ideas for dealing with management problems.

However, this book alone won't make you a leader. I have a friend who is a fitness fanatic. He buys all the magazines, is a member of a well-equipped gym and has an exercise bicycle in his bedroom. Yet the only exercise he gets is when he lifts the piles of health and fitness magazines from bedside table to bookcase. He tells me he really will do some exercise – but he just does not have time right now. And he always seems to have something more important to do. He wants the health and well-being that exercise will bring him, but without doing the work.

Bearing this in mind, if you are ready, I invite you to step out on the first stage of the leader's journey.

ACKNOWLEDGEMENTS

First of all I would like to acknowledge John Grinder and Richard Bandler, the co-developers of NLP, Robert Dilts, who has taken it forward in so many new and interesting directions over the years, and the many others involved in developing NLP.

My thanks to Carole Tonkinson and Elizabeth Hutchins at Thorsons.

Complexity theories were first developed mainly by Stuart Kauffman, Brian Arthur, John Holland and Chris Langton at the Santa Fe Institute. I believe their brilliant insights into the nature of complex systems will be increasingly recognized and applied to organizational leadership and self development. I have also been fortunate to 'listen' to many fascinating conversations about systemic thinking and complexity on the Internet, and would particularly like to thank Uri Merry, Ben Kutz, Mark White and Michael Lissack for provoking my thinking in many interesting directions. The mosaic I have made from it is, however, mine.

Finally, I thank my friends throughout the world for their help and encouragement: Alexandre de Faria, Brian van der Horst, Alix Louise von Uhde, Gill Norman-Bruce, Joey Walters, Drake Zimmerman, Bent Hansen, Erum Imran, Colonel Rashid Iqbal Khan, Gulsun Zeytinoglu, Vitor Caruso, Tim Murphey, Leo Anghart, Deborah Epelman, Gajic Zorica, Roman Braun and Oscar Caceres.

Credits
I have done my best to track down and credit the sources of the material in this book. Please let me know by mail if I have inadvertently omitted an important source or if you feel someone is not properly acknowledged. I will correct future printings.

STARTING THE JOURNEY

First Steps

Why do you want to develop as a leader? What do you want to achieve? A leader is going somewhere. Why move if you are happy with what you have?

We move for only two reasons: either we are unhappy where we are and want to be somewhere else, or we sense something better and are drawn towards it. However good our life, we get used to it and then we want more; our imagination always soars beyond our present state. The energy to start comes from our conviction within, coupled with a push from the outside. This call to adventure and the urge to play with the unknown has given us our art, music, science and commerce.

Leadership comes from our natural striving to constantly reinvent ourselves. You do not need external permission to be a leader. Nor do you need any qualifications or position of authority. Leadership does not depend on what you do already. Many people in positions of authority are not leaders; they may have the title but not the substance. Others have the substance, but no title. Leadership comes from the reality of what you do and how you think, not from your title or nominal responsibilities. Leadership blooms when the soil and climate is right, but the seed comes from within. So the only permission you need to begin is your own. The moment you say to yourself, 'I can be a leader,' you have already rolled up the map, put on your boots, got up from your easy chair and taken the first step on the journey.

Irish folklore tells the story of a group of tourists enjoying a walk in the countryside. They had a map, but even so, by early afternoon, they found themselves lost. The sky clouded over, the wind whipped the leaves around their feet and the first spots of warm rain began to fall on their faces. They decided to make for Roundmarsh, which, according to the map, was the nearest town. After an hour, unable to see through the curtain of rain, they decided to ask for directions. Walking on for half a mile, the rain eased off and they met a local man walking his dog in the opposite direction.

'Excuse me,' said the tourist leader, 'we are a little lost. Can you tell us how to get to Roundmarsh?'

The man stared into the distance at nothing in particular and considered the question very seriously.

'Roundmarsh?' he muttered. 'Roundmarsh? Hmm. That's a problem. If I wanted to get to Roundmarsh, I wouldn't start from here.'

It is always easier to get to where you are going when you know where you are. In the words of Max de Pree, the retired CEO of Herman Miller, 'A leader's task is to define reality.' The leader puts a stake in the ground and says, 'Here we are, what is possible?' Two thousand years ago, a Chinese proverb gave much the same soundbite: 'Gain power by accepting reality.' The ancients steal all our best ideas. But accepting reality by knowing where you are is the first step of every journey.

We need to ask three basic questions:

Where are we going?
Why are we going there at all?
How do we want to get there?

Then, as this is a leadership journey, we need to ask more questions:

What resources do we have to help us?
What are our limits and our strengths?
What traps do we need to avoid?
What do we know about leaders?
Who are they and what do they do?

What kind of models do we have for leadership?
Do we have a good map?

Why start the journey anyway? What prompts you? What draws you to being a leader? Unusual circumstances? A personal crisis? Perhaps a person has come into your life and changed your thinking. We all have defining moments in our lives and often a person will act as a leader for you. Sometimes we recognize it at the time, but not always.

I remember a seminar I attended a few years ago with Eloise Ristad, a marvellous teacher who was Professor of Piano at Colorado University. She gave workshops on music and performance anxiety, a big problem for many classical musicians. They are expected to give a flawless performance, 'speaking' with their instrument, which needs constant practice to master. The pressure can reduce solo instrumentalists to glassy-eyed paralysis, like a rabbit caught in the glare of a car's headlights. Musicians are taught to play their instrument at college, but they are given little guidance on how to perform it. Eloise had written a book called *A Soprano on her Head*[1] which I admired very much. She had a unorthodox approach to teaching music, in which she used all sorts of ways to interrupt performers' stuck patterns. The title of the book came from the way she cured a singer of stage fright. She asked this singer (who was tongue tied in her presence and could hardly croak a note) to stand on her head and then sing. Ridiculous! And yet it worked. You might say it gave her a whole new perspective on singing. It was certainly the beginning of the resumption of her interrupted singing career.

I remember coming back from that workshop thinking, 'I can write a book too.' The fact that I had not written anything beyond school essays at that time didn't seem to matter. A year later the manuscript was finished and it started me on a journey as a writer.

The call is when you suddenly recognize you want to change. One of my friends told me his turning point. He was with a textile firm, in name a manager but in reality a glorified clerk. His boss seemed to know less and work less than he did, and he referred to his in-tray as 'Hell' because it seemed to be a bottomless pit of torture and was always full. His out-tray was 'the ocean' because it was impossible to empty. Quite appropriately, the depth of Hell was how the boss decided what sort of worker you were. One Wednesday morning, after a longer than usual drive to work through the rush-hour traffic, a client blamed my friend loudly and publicly for something he knew nothing about. 'That's it!' he shouted as he slammed the telephone down. 'I'm leaving!' And he did, after tipping the contents of his in-tray on his manager's desk. He started his own business, where he earns less than he did before, but he is immeasurably happier, joining the ranks of the self-employed who have a tolerant and sometimes indulgent employer. He refers to that Wednesday as 'the day that all Hell broke loose'.

It can be a chance remark from a friend can set you searching, or a new project at work, a manager who becomes a mentor, moving house, starting a romantic relationship, becoming a parent. In the popular rendition of chaos theory, a butterfly flapping its wings in Beijing can conceivably cause a hurricane in Texas, such is the complexity, interconnectedness and unpredictability of the world's weather system. (If it worked the other way round, that would be the real miracle.) Our social relationships are at least as complex as the weather, so I have no trouble believing that a few words from someone in the right place at the right time can totally change your life.

You are called – to what? Let us look at this enigmatic quality 'leadership' more closely. The word deceives us in its simplicity. It does not mean the same for everyone. Ideas about leadership and what constitutes a good leader have changed throughout history. They also differ from culture to culture. For example, the American individualistic and challenging style of leadership is very different from the Japanese style of leadership. A good leader in Japan seeks consensus; they call it *nema washi*, meaning 'digging around the roots'. The phrase comes from the practice of cutting around a tree a few weeks before you want to move it. The cut roots start sprouting new growth, so when they move the tree, new growth takes hold straight away. The cutting also prepares the tree more gradually for the move than uprooting it in one go. But if they find too many roots, that is, a host of objections, Japanese leaders tend to withdraw and continue discussions. They will not usually bring an issue to a vote until they feel that most people will agree. The debate is over before the meeting.

Whatever their style, something that all leaders share is influence. We may see influential people on television, in films, in politics or at work, meet them socially or read about them in the press. We may admire them and want to copy them because they get things done, they stand for something important, something we want to be part of. We bestow 'leadership' on them. So leadership does not exist as an independent quality; it only exists between people. It describes a relationship. 'Followers' are the other half of leaders. They go together.

Leadership has long been associated with authority – we tend to concentrate on the leader, to think of them as innately superior in some way, and take the followers for granted. But formal authority is only one possible part of leadership. Many leaders do not have it. In some cases, perhaps 'companionship' better describes the relationship between leader and followers.

As leadership connects people in this way, I do not think it can be fully modelled from the outside by giving lists of how leaders act, culled from the study of other leaders. It can only be modelled from the *inside*, by each of us developing the values, beliefs and qualities we need to realize and achieve our purpose in life, to bring out our vision of what is possible. Then others will join us. We will be leaders first to ourselves and then to our companions.

Thought Experiment 1

How do you think of 'leadership'? What comes into your mind? Try it now.

What are the qualities of your mental picture?
Is it still or moving?
How far away does it appear to be?
Is it in colour or black and white?
Are you in the picture?
How do you feel about your picture?

'Leadership' an abstract noun and for many people the word conjures up a still picture, a frieze of troops on the battlefield or sometimes a symbol.

Now think of 'leading'.

What comes into your mind?
What are the qualities of your mental picture now?
How are they different?
How do you feel about this picture?

'Leading' is a verb and that means action, movement. Your mental pictures can spring to life.

When you think about 'leadership', remember the reality behind the word – leaders *act*. They move towards something. They excite action; they transform people and change how they think. Leadership as an abstract noun languishes as a theoretical concept with no life or movement – interesting, but kept safely at arm's length like a museum exhibit.[2]

Think of a leader. Who comes to mind? A military leader like the Duke of Wellington, Napoleon, Winston Churchill or General Schwartzkopf? A political leader like Tony Blair, President Kennedy, Margaret Thatcher or Bill Clinton? Or a religious leader like Christ, Mohammed and the Buddha? What of the humanitarian leaders like Mother Teresa and Albert Schweitzer, popular charismatic figures like Princess Diana, or film stars, music stars or top figures in the world of fashion?

Leaders form a very varied group, all strong characters who arouse passions both for and against. Yet they all have something in common that defines them as leaders – they have influence. They move people.

Vision

Leadership starts with a vision, a tantalizing glimpse of a possible future. A vision sounds very grand, but it has just two simple qualities: it inspires you to act, and involves and inspires others to act as well.

We all have our individual visions; leadership is about taking those and developing them into something greater, more fulfilling and more influential. We all try to shape the future by striving to make our dreams real. The question is, what dreams are you making real right now and are they really worthwhile? If you are not making your dreams real, why not?

Think of the future like a dark cave – Aladdin's cave. You wait, poised on the threshold. The cave goes back into the darkness, swallowing the shadows cast by the pool of light at the entrance. The atmosphere is full of possibilities; you hear stealthy sounds. You know both treasures and dangers exist here, but neither what nor where they are. Some objects in the cave are within easy reach and many people are content to stay at the entrance, happy with what they can take from the ante-room. But to find greater treasure you need to trust yourself to walk further into the cave.

There is no light switch here, only your ideas can provide the light to see further. You are the leader here. Perhaps there are others clustered by the entrance waiting to hear what you find, or create.

Aladdin's cave

Your ideas burn brightly for an instant, like a flare, and just for a second you and the others glimpse the riches around you and some of the guardians that you will have to overcome later. The flare dies and you rub your eyes, but the image persists in your mind, the impression stays with you. You know what you want and you know the direction in which it lies.

The initial flaring light has died down and become a torch, not so bright, but light enough to navigate by. People join you from the doorway and together you make your way into the depths of the cave. They light their own torches from yours as they go. Soon you have much more light, you can see further. No wonder more people are attracted to your band – you have plenty of light and you know where you are going. You make more detailed maps, the cave becomes more familiar. And still you have that first bright image in your mind that you can rekindle when the journey becomes hard and you meet unforeseen obstacles and guardians.

The cave changes while you move, you create new challenges, new pitfalls and new shortcuts by your advance. Sometimes you have to light another flare. You may be drawn deep into the cave, through fantastic landscapes. You may travel to the end of cul-de-sacs, or be distracted by superficially attractive but worthless trinkets at the side of the road, or even discover places you want to stay, but whatever happens you are committed to the journey, to going forward. You do not go back.

The same process powers our vision of a better life or a more competitive business. A leader always leads *somewhere*, even when the journey is inspired by a desire to get out of trouble. For example, 1992 was a disastrous year for the American retailer Sears, Roebuck and Company. They made a net loss of nearly four billion dollars, most of it in merchandising, on sales of just over 50 billion dollars. Sears was turned around spectacularly the following year by Arthur Martinez, who was head of the merchandising group, and in 1995 became CEO of the whole company. Starting from a simple vision statement of what was called 'the three Cs' – 'making Sears a compelling place to shop, a compelling place to work and a compelling place to invest' – the company went from the net loss of four billion dollars to a net income of 752 million dollars the following year, a sales increase of more than nine per cent. Of course the vision alone did not cause the turnaround – it was what they *did*, suggested, fuelled and guided by that vision. Vision guides action. Action changes the world in the direction of your vision.

There are no guarantees on the journey, however. Sometimes vision turns out to be a trick of the light, an illusion. What looked like a doorway turns out to be a dead end when you get close to it. Or the vision stands real and robust enough, but the leaders can't find the way, their strategy was mistaken and unfortunately there was only one chance. Sears took it and made it work, Apple computers did neither. Never it seems, has a company with so much good will managed so consistently to lose its way. In the late 1980s, Apple was a market leader in the computer industry with nearly 20 per cent of the world market in computer sales. In 1997, with debts of over one and a half billion dollars, it was a company struggling to survive. It was crushed under the Microsoft juggernaut, but poor leadership put it under the iron wheels in the first place. In 1998, it began a sales campaign with the slogan of 'Think different' and everyone hoped that it would take its own advice.

A journey starts when you see a difference between where you are and where you want to be, or to put it another way, when you no longer want to be where you are. The worse the current situation, the more difficult the journey, but you can't stay put either. This was the situation that faced both Sears and Apple, and many other companies face such a dilemma every year.

Unless you have a clear destination, you may walk in a circle and come back to where you started from, only this time it will be worse. To avoid these circular tours, you need to move towards something better *and* you need to change the thinking that brought you into that problem situation in the first place – you need to 'think different' in Apple's engaging but ungrammatical phrase. For example, Sears thought of themselves primarily as a men's shopping store, but market surveys were showing that a significant number of decisions to buy Sears merchandise were made by women. So they changed the marketing approach and started new lines in clothes and cosmetics. The Sears catalogue was a national institution, it had been published for over 100 years, surely it was worth keeping? No. It was losing 10 million dollars a year, so it was scrapped. And Apple? They were justifiably proud of their 'insanely great' technology, and consistently refused to license it to the rest of the computer industry. They also targeted the educational system as one of their primary markets, even though the results of this policy were regularly disappointing. They believed in a closed system and in keeping control of their technology, not realizing that influence and success in the new economy are based on connecting with others, so they can develop your ideas and make them even more valuable. In the knowledge field, the more people use your ideas, the more valuable they become. Apple succeeded all too well at keeping control of their ideas and thereby limiting their spread. The prize was hollow, because its value declined. Strategic decisions about what to license were being made by the engineers, who did not have the strategic vision to see where the market was heading. If ever there was a place to apply the saying 'a leader sees where everyone else is going and gets in front of them', this was it. Apple saw where everyone else was going and stayed put where they were, believing that others would have to come back to them. No one had to because they were on their own. They recapitulated the error of Sony in the 1980s with their videocassette technology called Betamax. It was generally seen to be superior to its rival VHS, but Betamax was a closed standard and VHS an open one. VHS became dominant in the industry and Betamax faded.

Sharing your Vision

So, not only do you need a good road map when you lead or follow a vision, but you must also allow your experiences and observations to refine it as you go along, and you must be able to share it with others. A leader creates a vision with others, or shares their own with others, and inspires them. A shared vision takes shape.

While 'a shared vision' sounds rather grand, the vision itself can be as splendid or as modest as you like. It does, however, have to be achievable, worthwhile and inspiring, first for yourself, and if you want to be a leader, for others too. If it inspires you alone, then you are at best a visionary and at worst a crank or an eccentric.

How do you make your a vision practical and achievable? First it has to be elaborated, refined and made more specific. Consider the following questions:

rtant to us?
or guiding principles.
want to accomplish?
ition or ultimate purpose.
How do we want to accomplish it?
The important goals and capabilities needed to achieve the vision.

Objectives are measurable steps on the way to those goals, they are targets that you must meet to achieve the goals. Objectives need to be measurable, so you have to decide what to measure, how to measure and how accurately to measure. Tasks are the work you have to do to achieve these objectives.

Vision

Purpose

Values

Goals

Capabilities

Measurable objects

Tasks

So, a vision is not a detailed blueprint, it's a direction, a combination of what you want and what you value. From this vision you naturally set your goals. Goals are dreams with deadlines. From the goals come a number of measurable, smaller objectives. Also, to achieve your purpose you will need certain qualities, and your values will guide the whole journey.

Vision

A vision answers significant questions, those that can only be answered by action:

What do I want to accomplish in my life?

What do I want to look back on having achieved?

If there were one great task I could accomplish immediately, as if by magic, what would it be?

What have I always wanted to do – that nagging thought that seems grandiose but will not go away?

What am I drawn towards doing?

These questions can give you the main purpose of your journey.

Leaders start with the vision that they think is achievable and worthwhile.

A fully elaborated and worked out and carefully worded vision is often called a 'mission statement'. To refine the vision into a mission statement you have to ask some critical questions, whether you are developing an organizational mission or a personal one:

Where are we going?

How will we get there?

What do we need to succeed?

What are our guiding values?

What will we measure for success and how will we measure it?

How long will it take?

Once you believe your vision to be achievable and practical, once you have your road map, you need to share it. How do you do this? You can write it down, you can talk to others, but the most powerful way of all is to live it and the values it embodies. Action can express a vision much better than words. Ralph Waldo Emerson, the American essayist and poet, put it this way: 'What you are doing speaks so loud I can't hear what you say.' People will always judge you first on what you do, then by what you say. Artists, designers and musicians all lead mainly by what they do.

To fully use your vision and share it with others you will at some point, however, have to find words that capture it in a clear and inspiring way. Inevitably the words will be less inspiring and your vision may lose force and be misunderstood. The world of pictures is evocative and lucid, the world of words is shadowy and full of double meanings. Sight takes in everything all at once, words give a little at a time. Try this experiment when you have a few moments to yourself. Look at your surroundings for a few seconds. Then close your eyes. Now describe your surroundings. It would take a long time, wouldn't it? But someone who knew the scene would recognize it from your first sketchy description. A vision statement in words has little meaning unless it can connect with and evoke the experience it refers to.

More difficult still, unlike your surroundings, a vision does not yet exist, it is an imaginary picture, like the form of a sculpture that only exists in your mind's eye. It becomes solid only as you work towards it. At first it's an outline. An evocative word sketch will allow people to create it in their own minds, to see it in their own terms. Then they will add to it, give it different perspectives and the vision will grow stronger. The more people share the essential vision, the more robust and multi-dimensional it becomes.

There is an art to putting a vision into words. The words need to be clear enough to capture the idea, yet vague enough for others to make their own meanings from it and enrich it. 'To put a man on the moon in 10 years' is one example of a vision. 'A family growing and being happy together' is another. 'A reliable overnight delivery service' is a third. How about 'Redefining what is possible in the media market'? The words need to be suggestive and evocative. To modify Einstein's famous dictum, 'Vision needs to be as simple as possible, but no simpler.'

I think it is natural to have a vision. It may be clear and central in your life. It may be hovering on the edge of your horizon – you may have a peripheral vision, as it were. Leadership takes that vision and puts it more fully into your life. You become more aware of it and start to act on it.

A vision can be about creating an international company, playing a leading role in your local community, being an inspiring manager, a top athletic coach, designing a killer software application, building a high-performance team or launching a new business project. It comes down to a simple question: what's worth doing?

Another question is, how long will the journey take? This depends on what you want to accomplish. Too short a journey and people are not stretched. They will not be interested if the end goal is too easy – no one needs a leader for an expedition to the corner shop. Too long a journey and there is too much tension – people will not even try, if the goal seems impossible. A leader skilfully stretches the distance just far enough to set up the right tension, but not far enough to strain or snap the link between the present and the future.

Suppose the journey has to be a long one? No business goes from sinking to soaring in less than a couple of years and if your vision is social change, that can take decades. The larger and more pervasive the change, the longer it takes. A long journey must embody something very important and be truly compelling for people to sign up. Alternatively, present conditions have to be very bad to get people moving. The leader must break a long journey into stages so it looks more manageable. No one climbs a mountain in one unbroken expedition, they welcome the resting points on the way to the top. The higher the mountain, the more breaks there are and the more comfortable they will be. Imagine looking up at a huge mountain and knowing you have to climb it in one trek. Your heart will sink to the bottom of your mountain boots. There have to be intermediate goals along the way or no one will even want to start in the first place. The leader will be left marching off into the distance on their own.

Exploring Mental Perspectives 1: Vision

It seems natural to represent time as distance in our minds. We talk of events 'far in the future' or 'close to the present' and the law of perspective operates in our minds as well as in the outside world. The longer a goal takes to achieve, the further away we represent it, and the further away, the smaller it seems. The smaller it seems, the less motivating and the less real it may feel, so why bother to start? Perspective is governed by an inverse square law. In other words, if you retreat to twice the distance from an object, it does not seem to become half the size, it becomes a quarter of the size – the size varies as a square of the distance. So the attraction a goal has for you will vary tremendously depending on whereabouts you put it in your mental field. A small distance can make a big difference.

Try this thought experiment. Think of something important you want to achieve in your personal or professional life. Imagine it in your mind. Make a picture of it.

Whereabouts in space is your mental picture? For example, it may be directly in front of you or to one side. You may be looking up at it or down on it.

How far away is it? Is it within arm's reach or further?

How long do you expect it will take to achieve?

Experiment by moving it further away. How do you feel about it now?

Does it seem more or less attractive?

Does it get smaller, larger or stay the same size as you move it further away?

Does the distance correspond to how much time you think it will take to achieve it?

Does it seem as though the further away it is, the further in the future it is?

Move it so far away that you can hardly see it. How do you feel about it now? Still motivated?

Now move it closer.

How does that change it?

Does it seem more attractive?

Does it get bigger, smaller or stay the same as you move it towards you?

Does it seem more achievable? Does it seem that you
    will get it any sooner?

How do you feel about it?

Explore whether you experience a threshold effect –
    a point beyond which your picture loses any attrac-
    tion. Also find the point where it is 'too close for
    comfort.'

Move your picture back to the most comfortable
    distance. Was that where it started?

Play with these distances. You will find them interesting.
If a goal ever seems unrealistic or not attractive enough
it may be too far away. The further away, the less clearly
you can see it.

    When you plan your goal, begin by making a picture
close to you and then move it to a suitable distance. Any
time you need to 'get in touch' with it again, pull it
closer.

Leaders make their goal seem possible however far into the
future it may be. One way to do this is to create a sense of
movement, for example:

'The day is approaching...'
'We can reach out and grasp...'
'Hitting a moving target...'
'We can reach it together...'
'It's within arm's length...'
'Headlong into the future...'
'Nothing can stop us...'

Leaders in Perspective

Mental perspective influences how leaders are perceived too.
Some leaders seem more accessible than others and this may
have to do with how closely we imagine them in our mind's
eye. Take the saying: 'A general commands, a good leader

leads and a great leader finds out where everyone's going and gets out in front.' A leader goes out in front, perhaps literally, certainly metaphorically. How far out in front should they be? Think about emotional distance. We talk about people being 'distant' and of 'staying in touch' and of 'hands on' management and 'close' friends and family. When a leader ventures too far ahead, the smaller they appear, and they get 'out of touch' and no longer understand the mood and feelings of those they are supposed to be leading. A distant leader can make the goal seem distant too.

Hierarchies create distance in another dimension, as we talk about a leader being 'above' their followers. In my view, vertical distance represents authority and horizontal distance emotional closeness or loyalty. A leader who has authority in a hierarchy can still be 'close' to their followers and many military leaders create fantastic loyalty in their troops because even the lowest ranks feel their commander understands them. It also helps if a leader has 'risen through the ranks'. Then they really are more likely to understand the concerns of the people they lead and it also gives them a credibility with their followers that an outside leader lacks. The more authority you have, the further up the hierarchy you are, and organizations with many levels of management risk creating too great a distance between the leaders and the followers.

We are not usually aware of how we think about leaders, but our view can affect how comfortable we feel about being a leader ourselves. If you think of a leader as large and looming over you, for example, you may feel uncomfortable about being a leader to others, because that would mean looming over them. When leaders are put on a pedestal, not only are their feet of clay more visible, but it's further to fall!

Consider what being a leader means to you. You will not want to go on the leadership journey if you believe that a leader has to be manipulative or superior.

Your ideas about leaders will be influenced by your experience of them. In 1997 I gave the first public NLP and business seminar in Prague in the Czech Republic, and the subject of leadership came up. I do not speak Czech so I had a translator and it soon became clear that the language did not have a word that adequately translated the concept that I was using the English word 'leader' to describe. They had two words: *manazer*, meaning 'an administrator', and *vudce*, meaning 'a Communist Party leader'. The seminar participants said a Communist Party 'leader' had no authority of their own (it came from Moscow), no vision (they did as they were told), little knowledge and was certainly no role model as they would consistently go home first at the end of the day's work! Such was the Czech cultural experience of their erstwhile Russian 'leaders' that we had to coin a new word to even begin to discuss the concept. In the end we decided to use the English word 'leader'. So a new word and a new concept entered the Czech language that day.

Our culture influences how we think of leaders. Some cultures, France for example, put more distance between leaders and followers. The social hierarchies are more pervasive. The greater the distance between leader and follower, the more difficult it seems to be a leader. You have further to 'climb' and more risks to take, because 'the nail that stands up gets hammered down'. In egalitarian cultures, such as America, the social landscape is flatter and leadership appears to be within the reach of everyone. It's possible for anyone to become US President (at least in theory, although a lot of cash helps).

Explore your own ideas about leadership with the following exercises.

Exploring Mental Perspectives 2: Leaders

Think of a person you regard as a leader.

How far away in your mental picture do they appear?
Change the picture to make them recede further into the distance. Do you feel any differently towards them now?

Make them further and further away. How do your
feelings change about them as a leader? Is there a
threshold point where they do not seem to be a
leader any more?

Put them back as they were and now bring them
closer to you. How does that change your feelings
about them? Is there a threshold where they are too
close and it feels uncomfortable?

Put them back at a comfortable distance. Now notice
how high the leader stands relative to you. Make
them higher than you. Do your feelings change?
What is it like as you make them higher and higher
above you?

Now move them below you. How does your feeling
about them change? Do you still think of them as a
leader? Is there a threshold where they do not seem
to be a leader any more?

Try these exercises with a number of different leaders.
Does the height and distance vary depending on who
you think of?

Leadership Exercise

A leader's influence comes from the relationship they
create with their followers. How we represent that relationship in our minds determines what we think of
leaders, how we respond to them and what sort of relationship we in turn create with others when we become
leaders.

Use this exercise to explore how you think about
leaders and how you see yourself as a leader.

Think of one or more people you respect as leaders.
Make a picture of them in your mind's eye. Imagine
people around them whom they influence and who
follow them.

When you think of these leaders in your imagination, where do you see them – in front of you, behind you or to the side?

In your mental picture, is the leader a long way in front, in the middle distance or a short way in front of the other people?

Is the leader larger, smaller or the same size as the people they are leading?

Are they above, below or on the same level as the people they are leading?

Does the leader seem more vivid, colourful or 'larger than life' than the followers?

If another person were to look at your picture, without knowing any of the people in it, how would they know which person was the leader?

How vivid is the picture?

Does it have colour?

Does it have movement?

Now listen for any sounds in your mental tableau. Are there voices?

Imagine the leader speaking. What quality does their voice have?

Now listen to the other people speaking.

What quality do their voices have?

Is there a particular voice quality that marks out the leader?

If a stranger were to listen to the voices without seeing the scene, would they be able to tell which voice was the leader's?

Now, keeping the rest of the picture the same, *see yourself* in the company of these leaders.

Make yourself the same size and distance as the leaders and put yourself in the same position relative to the other people as the leaders.

What does it feel like to see yourself standing there as
  a leader?
Adjust the picture until it feels comfortable.

Now step into the picture, be in your body, in the
  group of leaders, looking out through your own
  eyes at the people around who are following.

How do you feel there?

Metaphors of Leadership

How we see leaders in our mind shapes what we feel about
leaders, our relationship to them and, of course, how we
speak about them. Here are some examples:

'ahead of the field'
'on a pedestal'
'a cut above the others'
'close to the people'
'distant'
'out of touch'
'the common touch'
'in touch with the people'
'hands-on style'
'a towering leader'
'larger than life'
'head and shoulders above the rest'
'in a class of their own'
'stuck up'

If you catch yourself, or others, using these metaphors, you
can gain an insight into how you perceive leadership.

References

1 Eloise Ristad, *A Soprano on her Head*, Real People Press, 1982
2 The detailed qualities of our mental images, feelings and sounds are known as 'submodalities'. See Richard Bandler, *Using your Brain for a Change*, Real People Press, 1985, for a detailed discussion.

Bibliography

Bass, B., *Leadership and Performance: Beyond Expectation*, Consulting Psychology Press, 1985
Iacocca, L., and Novak, W., *Iacocca: An Autobiography*, Bantam Books, 1984
Kotter, J., *A Force for Change: How Leadership Differs from Management*, The Free Press, 1990

LEADERSHIP SUBSTANCE, STYLE AND SHADOW

Good leaders are ethical, responsible and effective. Ethical because leadership connects you to others through shared values. Responsible because leadership means self-development and not simply giving orders, however charismatically, to get others to do what you want. Effective because shared values and goals give the strongest motivation for getting tasks done. There are no guarantees, but this sort of leadership will bring you closer to people and give you the greatest chance of success.

Not all leaders are equally ethical, responsible and effective. There are differences in substance as well as style. Leadership also has a shadow side, as we shall see.

In the past we have often confused style with substance. A leader need not be a charismatic guru performing on stage to fanfares of music, treating their followers as if they were a game-show host. Such charisma is style, not substance; the guide at your side can be as influential as the sage on the stage. Lao Tse, the Chinese philosopher who lived in the sixth century BC, captured this aspect of a leader's work very nicely when he wrote, 'A leader is best when people barely know he exists. Not so good when people obey and acclaim him, and worse when they despise him. Fail to honour people and they will fail to honour you. Of a great leader, when his work is done, people say, "We did this ourselves." '

An effective leader leaves a legacy; they leave their footprints on the road for others to follow. A good leader develops themselves *and they develop others*. They bring people together rather than divide them. I read a striking example of this in a letter written by the Duke of Wellington to Lord Bradford at the British War Office in 1820. He says, 'I shall see no officer under my command is debarred, by attending to his first duty, which is, and always has been, to train private men under his command.'

Teaching others to be leaders makes sense on a personal as well as a business level. Parents are leaders in a family and they strive to help their children become independent adults. In business, leaders develop others in order to help them learn and help the organization become more competitive. Business is increasingly becoming knowledge based. What you know defines what you can do. Smart people build smart products. And smart people do not usually work in dumb organizations.

A perennial question about leadership is: 'Are leaders born or made?' And the answer is ... 'Yes.' Both. It's a misleading question because it is phrased as if the answer must be one or the other. We are all born with skills and talents and we have to make the most of them by learning. Shakespeare wrote, 'Some are born great, some achieve greatness and some have greatness thrust upon them.' No one leaps from the cradle a fully qualified leader. We all have to learn something. Only learning brings out our natural talents.

I am also suspicious of any single answer that closes the debate and takes away choice. For example, if you believe that leaders are born and not made, why try to develop yourself or others as leaders? The question has been answered in your genes.

In researching this book I read a great deal of literature on military leadership and not surprisingly, all of it states explicitly that leaders are made. On the other hand if you assume that leaders are made and a person's inherent character does not count, then you must concede that everyone is equally good as a leader in any situation, and we all know otherwise.

In my view, being a leader comes from a combination of who you are, your skills and talents, the relationship you create with others *and* your situation. Being a leader means working with these four core elements. The 'and' hides the magic in the equation. Understanding each piece of a jigsaw will not show you the picture until you put them together. Look for leadership in the whole, not in the pieces.

Unless we deal with that systemic aspect of leadership we have only 'laundry list leadership', a collection of factors that look good in theory, but do not connect in practice. The pieces may be the right ones but they won't do anything until they are joined, just as a television will not work with its bits strewn all over the floor.

So, to become a leader, develop yourself, your skills and talents, so you can lead by example. Develop your vision of where you want to go, so you can inspire others to come with you. Develop others and your ability to influence your companions and to evolve a shared vision between you. And develop systemic thinking skills to understand the situation, its limits and opportunities. I think these are the core skills of leadership.

> 'Analysing others is knowledge
> Knowing yourself is wisdom
> Managing others requires skill
> Mastering yourself takes inner strength.'

> *Tao Te Ching*

The Three Pillars of Leadership

What do leaders have that puts them at the forefront? And once there, what keeps them there?

Authority – the official or formal position they have.
Knowledge – what they know.
Example – their actions that inspire others to want to be like them.

These are the three pillars of leadership. A leader needs all three to stand firmly.

Authority

Our cultural thinking on leadership has been entangled in wars and battles and heavily influenced by military history. Say 'leader' and for many people a picture pops up of troops being led into battle (even though in most cases, the general in charge was at the back directing operations). This military metaphor still colours our view of business leadership and powers the 'command and control' management paradigm. It strikes deep. The world of sales is packed to the hilt with military metaphors. Managers talk of 'leading the troops into battle', 'fighting the price war' and 'a cut-throat market', as if the primitive urge to deal with the competition by bombing their boardroom and interning their sales people still appeals. No wonder sales people tend to suffer from battle fatigue known as 'burn out'. Any metaphor becomes destructive when taken too far and this one has had its day. 'Customer partnerships' should be what we hear now.

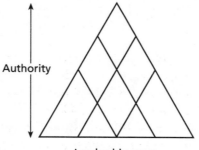

Leadership space

Leadership by authority

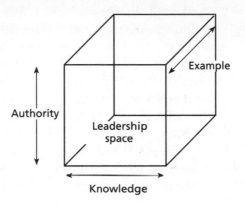

New leadership model

In a strict hierarchy like an army, high rank gives the possibility of leadership over those 'below' you, but authority alone falls short of leadership. Authority is not sensitive enough to context.

Managing, as already mentioned, used to be about planning and control. Top management decided what was to be done, middle management worked out how to do it and everyone else did as they were told. This model assumed, of course, that top management knew what needed to be done, that the orders had time to percolate their way down and that, like a good army, the lower ranks would obey.

This type of management would simply not work any more, even if we were still prepared to put up with it. Markets change fast and organizations have to react fast, so people in every part of the business need the knowledge and the permission to make decisions on matters that affect them. As organizations 'flatten out', lines of authority start to blur. 'Top' management no longer necessarily knows best. Information gives power, not the size of your office. Only change can be relied on.

The business writer and consultant Rosabeth Moss Kanter has beautifully summed up the situation: 'The mean time between decisions is greater than the mean time between surprises.' By the time you make a decision, based on what you know, the situation may have changed, and your decision may not fit the new conditions. Your business may be perfectly geared to solving yesterday's problems. What makes the difference is how quickly you can obtain and evaluate information. And the people on the spot are in the best position to do that. So now managers at every level need the confidence and skills to make decisions and to be able to foster those qualities in those they manage. They need to be able to manage knowledge. The new model of leadership fits in perfectly.

Even in the army, for example, appearances are deceptive. In critical situations of combat, team or project leaders are nearly always the most competent people for the job. They may be the highest ranking, but not necessarily so. The more dangerous the situation, the more competence rises over rank. In life or death situations, anyone who pulls rank over ability will lose. The lower the risk, the more formal authority becomes the normal way of operating. In no-risk conditions, during peacetime army training, say, the lines of authority are unquestioned. So even the army, with its vast tradition and publications on discipline and lines of command, recognizes that in a tight corner, the person best fitted to the job must lead. Leadership through knowledge takes over from leadership through authority.

The military metaphor of attack and defence does have a place, but in a strategic frame: outwitting and outflanking competitors in a battle of intelligence rather than big battalions. Survival of the fittest is a good description of how companies that adapt best to their environment survive and prosper (although 'survival of the fittingest' would be more accurate). Linked to this is the idea of co-evolution – businesses co-evolve, they do not evolve on their own, they change and influence each other in a network. No business changes in isolation – as one market opens, another contracts, and the winning strategy only wins as long as your competitor does not use it too. When they do, their reaction becomes part of the market situation and you need to change again. You have to react to others reacting to you reacting to others ... like a chameleon in a mirror, companies change according to the conditions, and the conditions change in response to the company policy.

Co-dependent, parasitic and symbiotic relationships occur in the business world as well as in the natural world. We talk of modern markets as a 'jungle', but look further and you will see commercial deserts and rain forests as well. Firms become dependent on particular suppliers and suppliers become dependent on firms. They need competitors to stimulate them. Microsoft would not have penetrated the Internet market without Netscape successfully leading the way. The so-called 'Browser Wars' (military again) that followed led to new software, as Microsoft changed its products to accommodate the Internet.

So, new patterns of products and relationships emerge from competition. Competitors naturally co-operate in a dance of new products and new markets: 'co-opetition'. The computer industry has the most obvious co-opetition – co-operation between competitors establishes technical standards, makes the market grow faster and creates new markets. At the moment Sun, IBM, Apple and Netscape have formed an alliance to challenge Microsoft's hold on the industry. Whoever 'wins', the game will go on.

A position of authority may help a person to be a leader, but a person in authority is only a leader if they have influence *apart* from their position. A good test of leadership is to consider whether, if a person suddenly lost their formal authority, others would still follow them. If the person is a leader, then yes. If not – maybe. If they were authoritarian, wanting unquestioning obedience and caring nothing for the people they led and were responsible for, then no, and their erstwhile followers might well turn on them to seek revenge for the humiliation they have suffered.

Authority works best where you have an accepted hierarchy, such as the army or the police force. Then people move together because of the strong implicit accepted values that everyone shares. If you are trying to lead people who do not share similar goals and values, then authority is not enough.

A report entitled *Liberating Leadership* was published by the Industrial Society in 1998. It was a survey of the views of 1,000 junior managers and professional staff. Of those surveyed, 81 per cent admired leaders who had no formal position of authority. They also made it clear they did not want the old command and control managers. They wanted managers who showed enthusiasm, supported their people and recognized individual effort. They did not like authoritarian managers who inspired fear and insisted things were done their way.

Authority alone is like pushing from behind. What automatic reaction do you have when pushed from behind? Resistance – unless you are travelling in that direction anyway and you experience the push as helpful. When you do not know what lies ahead and you are not sure whether you want to move forward, resistance is completely understandable.

Imagine a group of people all working together like a string of beads. Now imagine trying to get this loose collection of individuals to move forward together in the same direction by pushing them from behind. Even if you push evenly across the whole group, some may resist and the line will break up as some move forward while others drop behind. To keep the line in shape, traditional management exerts force from the side. The more people resist authority, the more management they need and more difficult to get anything done.

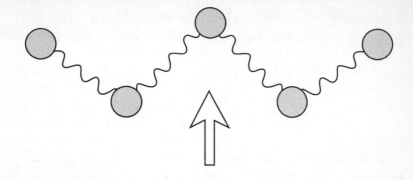

Now, imagine the same collection of loosely linked individuals being pulled forward. They all move together smoothly and need very little management from the side to keep them in shape. Authority alone pushes. Leadership *pulls*, because it draws people towards a vision of the future that attracts them.

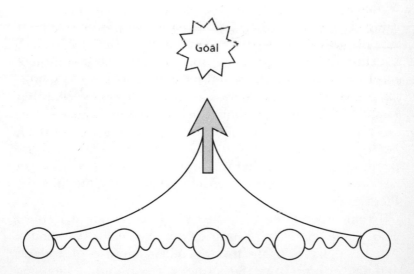

The difference between authority and leadership is the difference between a boss and a leader:

A boss has conscripts, a leader has recruits.
A boss has power, a leader has influence.
A boss depends on a position of authority, a leader gains
    authority by being themselves.
A boss can evoke fear and demands respect, a leader com-
    mands respect.
A boss says, 'I will,' a leader says, We will.'
A boss shows who is wrong, a leader shows what is wrong.
A boss knows how it's done, a leader knows how to do it.
A boss gets people to do things, a leader gets people to want
    to do things.
A boss drives their colleagues, a leader inspires them.
A boss is obeyed, a leader is followed.
And, before you have an argument with a boss, take a good
    look at both sides – his side and the outside!

Knowledge

Knowledge is the second pillar of leadership. You can be a leader by virtue of what you know. When my car breaks down, I take it in to the garage for repair. When my computer breaks down, I do what I can to fix it, but usually I call the support line. If I want to know about the latest fashion or music, I ask my teenage daughter. Mechanics, doctors, engineers, lawyers and teachers can all be leaders by what they know. And knowledge alone is insufficient.

Think of your best teachers or coaches, those who really made a difference for you and what you could do. Who comes to mind? A teacher from school? A college teacher, or a sports coach, or business coach? What sort of qualities did they have?

I remember when I was at college, there was a lecturer who would enter the musty lecture hall with its wooden benches polished by the trousers of a generation of students and deliver his lecturer for an hour in a monotone, looking down at his notes all the time. Then he would pack away his notes and leave. He barely looked at the class. We wondered if he would notice if no one was there for this weekly ritual. A group of us used to draw lots to decide who would attend in any one week and secretly record the lecture so we could all listen to it later. The only thing I remember about this man's lectures was that he pronounced 'food' as 'fud', which tells you how captivated I was. This man knew a lot about his subject, without ever inspiring me to find out anything about it above the bare minimum. Other lecturers were superb, stimulating and not only did I remember what they told me, but I also left the lecture hall wanting to find out more in my own time because the subject came alive when they spoke of it.

So knowledge will win over authority – would you rather be in the hands of someone who knows what they are doing or someone who has the formal authority in the situation? – but true leaders have something more. They give of themselves.

Example

Example is the third pillar of leadership, and the strongest. People look to a leader for ideas and guidance, and the strongest message comes not from what you say, but who you are.

A leader who acts as a role model takes responsibility for what they do. Responsibility is a double-edged word – the ability to respond is one edge, the recognition of your influence the other. Influence and responsibility go together. Your self, values, beliefs, expectations and actions enter everything you do and affect everything you do, and if you pay attention to your experience, then what you do affects you and changes you and the people with you. A responsible and effective leader does not think of themselves in isolation. They are part of the team they lead. This means that they lead and influence both themselves and others.

In order for leaders to act as role models and lead by example they have to be true to themselves. In doing this, they give us the message not to be like them, but to be ourselves, a message we all recognize. And in being true to ourselves we are developing our own leadership qualities, moving further along the path of leadership.

Being a leader is not always easy, though, and there are no facile answers. Most choices are vague, fuzzy and cannot be *logically* argued one way or another. I have a favourite Sufi story about the holy man Nassr-U-Din presiding as a judge in a civil court where two people were disputing a grievance. The first man argued his case very eloquently.

'That was very convincing!' said Nassr. 'You are obviously right!'

'A moment, sir,' whispered the clerk of the court. 'You must wait for the other man to argue his case before deciding.'

The second defendant took the stand and presented his case no less eloquently.

'Of course!' said Nassr. 'I must have been blind. Now I see that you are right!'

The clerk pulled at his sleeve. 'But my lord,' he hissed, 'they can't *both* be right!'

'No,' said Nassr. 'You're right.'

Sometimes both ways seem right and yet we have to choose one or the other – a difficult decision. In such cases we have to follow what we trust. The word 'trust' comes from the same root as the word 'truth'. Truth for each of us is what we trust. If we do not trust ourselves, then 'truth' becomes what others tell us. Ultimately, leadership means trusting yourself and developing others to trust themselves. People do not trust those who do not trust themselves.

Leadership Style

Different leaders will have different mixtures of knowledge, authority and example. A teacher can be a leader by virtue of what they know and the position they hold. A leader may be someone with formal authority – a manager, an army officer, police officer, or elected official. A leader may have religious knowledge and authority. You cannot set yourself up as a role model, that position, like leadership, is one others have to give you, and it may be unwelcome. We have all taken parents and significant adults as role models when we were children. When we have children we automatically become a role model for them, whether we want it or not.

A coach can be a leader. The British tennis player Greg Rusedski went from fifty-sixth in the world rankings to sixth in a few months under the guidance of his coaches, first Brian Teacher and then Tony Pickard. Rusedski is a talented player and his coaches were able to inspire him to play to his talent. Great athletes lead by example and they usually have great coaches – who are leaders of a different sort. Coaches in business help a colleague solve a problem or improve at a task through discussion and guidance. When coaching deals with personal issues and where the personal qualities of the coach become as important as their business skills, then coaching shades into mentoring. You may not be able to pick your coach, but you always choose your mentor.

A healer can be a leader, usually through the knowledge they have. Doctors and therapists are leaders when they lead people to greater health and well-being. Internal and external consultants can heal organizational rifts.

A steward, someone entrusted to guard what is important, is another kind of leader. In his book *Stewardship* (Berrett-Koehler, 1996), Peter Block writes of service in the cause of a larger vision, of accountability, and an end to a blame and control culture in the workplace. Much of this I would apply to leadership. I use stewardship in a more limited sense: as a style of leadership.

The steward's role as a guardian of what is important and worth keeping is important, for example in business, for although businesses must continually renew themselves, too much change is as bad as too little. Without any change a company will freeze and stagnate into an uncompetitive dinosaur, but with too much change the company risks losing the valuable parts of its business. A steward identifies and preserves what is worth keeping, what keeps the company stable. That is successful change – keeping the good things about the present and letting go of the rest. Any leader must be a steward to some degree.

Sometimes a designer is a leader. Designers shape our lives. Look round you and remember that all the man-made objects you see – buildings, furniture, clothes, cars and other machines – first began as ideas. Good designers lead the way in architecture, interior design, fashion and household appliances while others follow. You may never have met the architect who designed your house, but they influence your life every day. Leaders of fashion influence our choice of clothes, furniture, the music we listen to and the books and newspapers we read.

Finally there are those leaders who simply provide a role model. Think of the people who have influenced you the most. They may have been in authority. They may have had more knowledge than you. But there was probably something extra – something personal. They embodied values you admired.

I think a leader is also like a hero. The derivation of the word 'hero' is interesting. It means 'to protect and serve'. Usually the word conjures up ideas of courage, saving lives, maybe winning medals for valour or overcoming impossible odds. But all heroes, even those from Hollywood movies, have another, inner task – they have to overcome a dragon in themselves, they have to go beyond themselves and develop the qualities they need to overcome their task. There is one sure way of telling the hero in a story – the person who has learned the most, the person who is changed the most at the end. Both Luke Skywalker and Darth Vader are heroes in the *Star Wars* series of films. They were not heroes at the beginning, but they became so by how they responded to the challenges they faced. So becoming a leader means undertaking both an outward and an inward journey – to accomplish something worthwhile in the outside world, to inspire others in a worthwhile task and to discover inner resources that you did not know you had, to become a leader in your own way.

Leadership Style

Where in your life do you already have a leadership role?
In what area of your life do you have authority, either formal or informal?
Where do you have greater knowledge than others?
Where do you provide a role model for others?

In these areas you are already a leader. How could you become even more influential?

Do you have the role of a teacher?
Where do you give others knowledge and skill?
Are you a designer? Where do you shape others' lives by what you make?
Are you a coach? Where do you try to bring out the best in others?
Are you a healer? Where do you help others who are hurt in mind or body, or where do you bring people together and make them feel good? (A negotiator is also a kind of healer.)
Are you a steward? Do you keep important values or objects safe in times of change?

What aspect of leadership particularly appeals to you?
How could you develop more of this in your life or expand what you already have?

What matters to you about being a leader?
Why do you want to develop as a leader?
What will that get for you?

The Shadow Side

'Power tends to corrupt and absolute power corrupts absolutely.'

Lord Acton

All virtues flip into vices when taken to extremes and leadership is no exception. Leaders must develop others to become leaders, otherwise leadership can sink into a self-serving authority, where power becomes its own justification. All types of leaders face this danger.

The dark side of the authoritative leader is an authoritarian leader. An authoritarian leader demands unquestioning obedience and in order to achieve it must either undermine their followers' self-trust, so that they cannot think for themselves, or threaten dreadful consequences for disobedience. In extreme cases, authoritarianism dehumanizes the followers – they become instruments of the leader and not people in their own right. Unquestioning obedience is always suspect except in exceptional situations such as armed combat and even then higher values of shared humanity continue to operate – obeying orders has never excused war crimes. In business, 'boss' is shorthand for an authoritarian leader.

Coaches work with colleagues to help them and improve their performance. The dark side of a coach is a jehu – a wonderful word that means 'a furious driver' and conjures up a picture of a charioteer in the final stages of a chariot race, neck and neck with the next man, whipping the horses and everyone around him in his desperate frenzy to win. Coaches can turn into jehus when they try to fulfil their own unsatisfied needs through others, instead of trying to help them achieve the best they can in their own terms. They blur the boundaries between themselves and others and do not own their own striving. They turn people into slaves.

A healer has patients who need their help. The dark side of the healer is the quack – someone not so much interested in helping people as in making fame and fortune from the remedies they peddle.

Likewise a steward who forgets that he guards in service of renewal and development becomes a jailer, holding onto the past, blinded to the present and the future by the ghosts of antiquity. A steward makes you a guest; a jailer makes you a prisoner of their prejudice, rooted in the past.

A designer is a leader through the skill and knowledge that they put at the service of their public. They will have apprentices who study their work and gain skills to design in their own way. A designer who forgets that their success depends on pleasing others and ignores the wider community becomes a prima donna. They may indulge themselves and forget that they are only leaders because of the value they create for others. Such a designer loses touch with their public and needs an uncritical audience who will follow their whims regardless and imitators who will copy the designs rather than learn the design skills and then use them to create something that expresses their own personal vision.

Then there is the role model who suffers from delusions of grandeur and acts as if they are specially favoured and above those who admire them. Paradoxically, as soon as they do that, they lose their value as a role model. We pick role models for who they are and what they can teach us, not who they believe they are. A person cannot be a role model on their own, they can only be chosen as a role model. So once they think of themselves as role models irrespective of their followers, they lose touch with reality and create an artificial self that they then have to maintain at any price. Although this is a false self, in a final ironic twist they may then depend on it for self-esteem. So they want worshippers or clones who can feed their image, rather than real self-knowledge.

The shadows fall and the dark side of leadership creeps in when leaders lose touch with themselves and those qualities that made them leaders in the first place. First they demand their followers be blind to their weaknesses and then blind to their blindness. They become more concerned with keeping their power than with developing others. They may still influence others, but a leader who loses themselves will surely lose others as well.

The most extreme example of the dark side of leadership comes from a devious kind of authority sometimes called the 'guru syndrome'.[1] A guru is a holy man who serves as a spiritual guide and source of enlightenment in Eastern spiritual traditions. Genuine gurus are honourable leaders of the best kind. However some people set themselves up as quasi-gurus, promising their followers inner and outer freedom – but only at the price of inner and outer slavery. Their message is 'Depend on me to be free!' These are bigots, not gurus. They want obedience and compliance from their followers and they usually claim that their way is the only way. Their demands are as authoritarian as those of the most rigid hierarchical military organization. They gain power by eroding the self-trust of their followers, who then cling to them for certainty. Real leaders never demand a person's self-esteem and self-trust, they seek to *increase* it. They develop others, they do not impoverish them.

Leaders have power in the sense of having the ability to get things done. There is another, darker side of power – power over other people: a one-way passage of influence that ignores the other person's freedom of response. Influence is universal – we all influence each other, we cannot stop ourselves. To be alive is to be influencing and influenced. Most influence is random and purposeless. Leaders use their influence for good effect and their followers allow themselves to be influenced through the shared vision of where they want to go, while also in turn influencing the leader. But sometimes a leader's attempt to maintain power becomes more important than the vision that inspired it and the tasks needed to reach it. Such a leader will try and manipulate people, to get them to do things that are not in their interests. No one likes to be manipulated, but some people allow it because they need someone to take responsibility for them.

Many leaders create hierarchies, or find a position in a hierarchy, usually near the top. Hierarchies are not bad, but mostly useful ways of structuring power and authority, and are a natural means of organizing people working together while maintaining clear accountability. Hierarchies alone, however, tend to be rigid. They need to be balanced by small groups or self-organizing teams that bring innovation and creativity into an organization.

However, when an authoritarian power-driven hierarchy tries to maintain power rather than move toward its vision and carry out the shared tasks it was set up to do, then we have a cult. 'Cult' usually describes a religious or quasi-religious group, but I like to use the word more widely to describe any power-driven authoritarian group.

A cult has no external checks on the leader, no appeal against their judgement, no way out without losing everything the members have accomplished in the cult. The shadow guru, meantime, behaves above the law they profess to administer, above the vision they expound. They set their needs above those of everyone else in the group. They apply a law but count themselves above it. Such leaders have to be regarded as perfect and right, because the followers' self-respect depends on it. The more bizarre the doctrine, the more they have to believe it or lose everything, so they often defend the leader without knowing the facts. The leader has to be right. Newspapers sometimes expose so-called 'spiritual leaders' that live the life of utmost luxury while their disciples are delighted to give up what little they have for their leader. In the worst and most tragic circumstances they can even be persuaded to give up their lives.

Cults are power driven. They are also exclusive, an in-group with a clear impermeable boundary. They separate from non-members. They limit free-thinking and action among members, sometimes even to the point of controlling areas that have nothing to do with their vision, such as what food members can eat, what people they can talk to and what clothes they can wear.

A community, as opposed to a cult, is a group of people who come together freely to achieve a common goal driven by a shared vision. Everybody participates and the boundaries are not rigidly controlled. Communities not only tolerate, but value diversity. They also usually permit what they do not prohibit, while cults prohibit what they do not permit.

Community to cult is not a sharp 'either/or' distinction, but a continuum. Groups range from one extreme to the other, but cultish elements always come from the dark side of leadership and a shadow leader will start to crystallize a cult around them.

There are some basic questions that will show up the difference between cult and community:

What is the purpose of the group?
What is its vision?
How does the group decide what to do?
Does the leader have the only vote?
How is power distributed?
Does power only flow from top to bottom or are there checks?
To what extent do all members have a say in what happens?
Does membership of the group constrain what the members can do?
Does it set limits on who they can associate with?
Does it set limits in their life in areas that have nothing to do with the common tasks of the group?
Does the group create self-trust or self-distrust in its members? Are they made dependent?
How easily can they leave?
How responsive is the group to feedback from outside?
Is there one truth or are many points of view taken into account?

Leadership and Relationship	
Type of Leadership	Dark Side
Authority ... recruit	Boss ... conscript
Coach ... colleague	Jehu ... slave
Teacher ... student	Pedagogue ... stooge
Healer ... patient	Quack ... victim
Steward ... guest	Jailer ... prisoner
Designer ... apprentice	Prima donna ... imitator
Role model ... follower	Idol ... wannabe
Guru ... disciple	Bigot ... proselyte
Leaders build community	Bigots build cults

The difference between good leadership and its dark side comes from the type of relationship that leaders build.

There are in fact three relationships:

First the relationship between the leader and the followers. Leaders build a relationship of trust and self-development. Shadow leaders build a relationship of dependence and submission.

Secondly, the relationship between the followers. Good leaders build a relationship of trust and equality. Shadow leaders build distrust and fatalism.

Thirdly, the relationship between the group and others who do not share their goals or vision. Good leaders keep the boundaries open. Shadow leaders close the borders.

Pacing and Leading

When you want to lead others, either professionally or in your personal life, you have to start by acknowledging where they are and what is true for them. Where are they starting from? In NLP this is called 'pacing'.

You pace others by meeting them first of all in their world. You try to understand what matters to them, how they experience the world, without trying to change it. Because you confirm what is true for them, you begin to build trust. Pacing establishes the initial bridge. Once you have done that, then you can lead them.

Pacing and Management

Management is the equivalent of pacing an organization. Management aims to achieve consistent, orderly results in the short to medium term, while controlling the present. Leadership makes the future.

Management versus leadership is a hollow debate – organizations clearly need both. They need day-to-day stability that management gives *and* the innovation and renewal that leadership promises. Weak management with weak leadership will put a company out of business very quickly. Strong management and weak leadership will keep a company running for some time, but eventually it will fade, because it will be adapted to the past. In more forgiving times, when the pace of change was slower, a business could get by for years like this, and many did. But it is not possible now. This doesn't mean that all managers have to turn into leaders, but it does means that people have to take on a leadership as well as a managerial function.

Good leadership and poor management, on the other hand, is an exciting roller-coaster ride, but it doesn't usually last long. Bursting with vision, a business will flare, flourish and fade in a short space of time. Business needs a good balance of management and leadership to prosper and keep prospering.

We need to distinguish between the role of manager and the activity of management. 'Manager' is a job title. A person with such a title can lead as well as manage. Organizations have not got around to establishing 'leader' as a job title in its own right (except in an informal and ironic way), but we do have team leaders, so the role and activity is becoming recognized.

Management keeps existing systems running smoothly. It is a skill; leadership more an identity issue. Leaders innovate, they change or modify existing procedures, and they focus on transformation. Leaders motivate people through their beliefs and values, pushing the edges of the current organizational culture; management accepts the current organizational culture and makes it work. Management gets people to do things and leaders get people to want to do things. Management works within boundaries and leaders work with boundaries (not without boundaries!) Managers are people who do things right. Leaders are people who do the right thing.

The difference between management and leadership is nicely captured by the story of two guides directing a party of sightseers through a dense forest. One is busy with the maps, finding the best route, pointing out the different sorts of trees and generally keeping the party together. 'Let's keep going!' he shouts. 'We're on the right track.' The leader, however, has wandered off ahead and, after looking around, has climbed a tall tree just ahead of the party. He looks out over the landscape and shouts down, 'Hey! We're in the wrong forest!'

Pacing in Organizations Leading in Organizations

Manager	Leader
Seeks control	Facilitates change
Keeps procedures going	Makes new procedures
Does things right	Does the right things
A set of skills	A set of skills and an identity
Mainly at the neurological level of skills	Mainly at the neurological level of identity
Administration	Innovation
Get people to do things	Get people to want to do things by appealing to values and beliefs

Your Leadership Credentials

Leaders are realists, they are inspired by what they want, but they also have a grasp of what is happening all around them. Leaders who do not pace current reality become idealists, fired by what should happen, but mostly ineffectual in making the changes they want, because they do not accept the present. Again the Chinese proverb comes to mind: 'Gain power by accepting reality.'

Do this now at the start of your leadership journey by extending yourself the courtesy of pacing yourself. Find out what is true for you now. This means building a leadership cv listing all your present skills and resources.

We will do this using a descriptive framework known as 'neurological levels', developed by the NLP trainer Robert Dilts from the work of Gregory Bateson.[2] There are four levels: environment; behaviour and the associated skills; beliefs and values; and finally identity.

The first level is the environment: the where and when of our lives, the places and the people – your surroundings, fixtures, fittings, office, technology and everyone you work with. In a wider sense, the environment means the context, the whole situation. The environment makes a context as pieces make up a system – they form a unique figuration that either helps you or limits you.

The second level is behaviour: what you do, all your actions and the associated skills. Some skills we take for granted – reading writing, thinking and talking, for example. Once upon a time we put a great deal of effort into learning these, but now they form the background to our lives. We have many other skills that we do not appreciate because we take them for granted. Some we learned formally, for example mathematics, music, teaching, typing and driving a car. This level also includes personal qualities, for example optimism, determination, rapport, decision-making, coaching and flexibility. These are all skills, ways of using our minds that produce these results.

The third level is that of beliefs and values. Leaders operate here. Beliefs are the rules we make for ourselves and assumptions we have about what is possible and, therefore, what can happen. Leaders redefine what is possible. Values are what matter to you, those things you hold dear. They may be feelings like love, commitment, well-being or confidence. Good health matters to most people. Beliefs and values guide our actions, they determine what capabilities we have, because we will not spend time on something that is not important to us or that we believe will not help us.

Businesses have values as well, guiding principles that determine how that company does business. There may be formal rules, enshrined in such things as employee charters, customer charters and various sorts of mission and vision statements. Every business also has an informal culture: what really happens, how the formal values get put into practice (or not). Informal and formal values can differ greatly.

Beliefs are those ideas we take as true and use to guide our actions. We all have beliefs about what sort of people we are and what we are capable of. These beliefs act as permissions for or limitations on what we do. When we believe something is possible, we will try it; if we believe it impossible, we will not.

The fourth level is identity. Your individual identity is your sense of yourself as a person. It takes in your dearest values and beliefs. Your name marks your identity, while in the same way an organization has an identity expressed in its name and perhaps its logo. Sometimes the organization takes its identity and values from its founder or chair; the company may be identified with an individual in the public eye, like the Virgin group with Richard Branson. This can work powerfully in favour of an organization as long as the leader of the company is admired. Branson, for example, is seen as a creative and charismatic figure, and so Virgin appears as an innovative and energetic company.

Two levels beyond identity suggest themselves: the social dimension, and the spiritual level. If identity is about 'I', then these levels are about 'we'.

The first is about our social relationships, how we fulfil our responsibilities to others as members of our communities and culture, and how people combine their talents and diversity to form something greater than themselves. Communities are more than collections of people, they embrace all the other levels. Members of a community share an environment, have skills used for the good of all and share fundamental beliefs and values. At this level a business would look at how it relates to the wider community, particularly in terms of its ethical principles, public safety record, any pollution it causes and how it deals with the rights and feelings of minorities.

The spiritual level is how you experience your connection with humanity as a whole – what it means to be human, and your relationship with what is both beyond you and part of you. Here we enter the field of religion and spirituality.

Use the following questions in the neurological level framework to pace yourself – to explore the total of your present circumstances, friends, family, work and surroundings – drawing up your cv for being a leader. You may also want to explore what attracts you about leadership.

As you work through the questions, notice any doubts and difficulties that they trigger. Also observe at which neurological level they come up, but do not try to change them yet. Just acknowledge them as part of pacing yourself and take them as valuable information.

Environment
What are your present circumstances?
Where do you work and with whom do you work?
What is your day-to-day routine?
How will your environment be different when you are a leader?
Where do you want to be a leader?
Who will be affected and how?

Where are you most dissatisfied with your present
   situation?
Say to yourself, 'In certain circumstances, I can be a
   leader.' How do you feel about this statement?

Behaviour and Capabilities

What skills do you have? (Skills are anything you do
   well in any context. You probably take a lot of your
   skills for granted.)
What do people appreciate you for?
What do they praise you for?
What do they say you are good at?
What do you think you are good at?
What qualities do you have that are valuable?
   Count your education and specialized training and
   learning.)
What have you learned about human nature?
What communication skills do you have?
What professional skills do you use every day?
What skills do you have that you think are particularly
   useful for a leader?
Now imagine being your best friend. From that point
   of view, what uniquely special qualities do you see
   yourself having?
Where are you under-performing at the moment?
If you have people you manage already, where are they
   under-performing?
Say to yourself, 'I have the skills to be a leader.' How
   do you feel about this statement?

Beliefs and Values

What is important to you about being a leader?
What would you be able to accomplish as a leader?
What do you believe about leaders?
What sort of leader would you want to be?
Say to yourself, 'I can be a leader.' How do you feel
   about this statement?

Say, 'Leadership is important.' How do you feel about
that statement?
Say, 'It is important that I am a leader.' How do you
feel about that statement?

Identity

Do you think of yourself as a leader already?
What is it like to think of yourself as a leader?
How does being a leader fit with the sort of person
you are?
Say to yourself, 'I am a leader.' How do you feel about
this statement?
What sort of leaders do you understand best?

Connections and Community

Make up a relationship and network list. Imagine yourself in the middle of a space that contains all your
relationships. Imagine all the people you know, friends,
family, colleagues and acquaintances filling that space.[3]

Who is near you?
Your family will probably be closest. As you look
beyond them, who do you see? Your close friends?
Look further. There will be many people you have
known and have lost contact with, from school, college
or previous places you have lived. You may have
friends you know from e-mail but have never met.
How does it feel to be a leader in this community?

Beyond

How does being a leader fit into your spiritual life?

References

1 For an excellent analysis of the dark side of guru and religious leadership see J. Kramer and D. Alstad, *The Guru Papers: Masks of Authoritarian Power*, Frog Ltd., 1993.
2 See Robert Dilts, *Skills for the Future*, Meta Publications, 1993, or *Changing Belief Systems with NLP*, Meta Publications, 1990.

Gregory Bateson was an English writer and thinker on anthropology, cybernetics and psychology. He had wide interests and wrote on many topics. See his *Mind and Nature*, Fontana, 1980, and *Steps to an Ecology of Mind*, Ballantine, 1972.
3 Lucas Derks has done excellent detailed work on inner space representing social relationships. See his 'The social significance of inner space', *Social Panorama*, IE Publications, 1997.

Bibliography

Kanter, Rosabeth Moss, *The Changemasters: Innovation for Productivity in the American Corporation*, Simon and Schuster, 1983.

VISION AND VALUES

Values

What fuels your vision? The energy and the reason to move forward are provided by your values. Values are what matter to you. So, what is really important for you? Once you know that, your goals will begin to fall into place and you will have the energy to pursue them.

Start by knowing your own values, so you can lead yourself, then it will be easier to find out what matters to others, so you can lead them.

I suggest five broad categories in which to explore your values: personal development, relationships, work, health and leisure. You will probably find that values will overlap, because, for example, you develop yourself through work, and good health involves satisfying relationships and engaging work.

The next exercise will help you be clear about your values.

Personal Leadership Exercise 1: Your Values

Do this exercise when you have some time for yourself and will not be disturbed.

Make a list of the areas of your life where you want to clarify what is important to you, for example:
personal development
relationships
work

ealth
leisure

Pick one area to begin with, your work for example,
    and ask yourself:
What is important to me about work?
What do I look for in a job?
What keeps me in my work?
What five things help me do my job well?
Why are they important to me?
What five things do I like about my job?
Why are they important to me?
What would cause me to leave my present work?
What would I like to change about my work to make it
    more satisfying?

Then, choose some experiences in your work where
    you achieved something really worthwhile. What
    was important to you about those experiences?
What do they suggest about the kind of work you
    value?
What things do you value in work that money can't
    buy?
What do you value about the people you work with?

These questions will help you crystallize your values
about work. Aim to get three to five working values, but
don't try to put them in order. Values form a system,
not a hierarchy.

Clarify your values in each of the other areas –
personal development, health, relationships and
leisure – using similar questions. Add any other areas
that are important to you.

When you have your (at least) three values in each area, you
need to find out the rules you have about how and when
these values are fulfilled. What has to happen for you to
know these values are met? Also, what lets you know these

values are being disregarded? Part of being a leader is not only wanting our own values met but also acting from them and creating them for others – in their terms. Values are captured in rather vague words like 'recognition', 'friendship', 'fulfilment', 'joy', 'love', 'commitment' and 'well-being', but behind these fluffy concepts lie real experiences and they will be slightly different (sometimes very different) for each of us. When we have these experiences, they let us know that the value has been fulfilled. They are our reward.

Specific behaviour and experiences that we see, hear and feel and that are evidence of our values are called 'value equivalents' in NLP. There are four sorts of value equivalents:

- First, what do others have to do to meet your values? Different people need very different evidence for the same value. What one person regards as a fair salary, for example, another would regard as a pittance and a third regard as a fortune. For one person, competence means working out a task in advance and feeling they could do it if they needed to. For their neighbour, competence means the whole task finished perfectly to the satisfaction of someone else. Perhaps for one person, recognition means a warm hand on the shoulder and a heartfelt 'thank you' from their superior. For another, it is a mention in the staff newsletter and a salary bonus. Being loved for one partner in a marriage might mean being told, for the other it may be loving touches and caresses.
- Secondly, what do others do that violates your values? For some people dishonesty means stealing money, for others it is telling lies.
- Thirdly, how do you judge when you are acting from your own values? We do not necessarily apply the same rules to ourselves that we apply to others.
- And lastly, how do we judge when we are acting against our values?

owing exercise. It may give you some insights into
nal value equivalents.

Personal Leadership Exercise 2:
Evidence for Values

How do you judge when your values are fulfilled?

Take one category, work for example, and look at
each of the three values you found in the earlier exercise.

Ask yourself, 'What has to happen for me to know
this value is being met?'

Think back to a time when you felt that value was met
– a 'reference experience' for that value. What happened that gave you that satisfaction?

Now think about what has to happen for you to know
that a value has been disregarded. You probably have a
reference experience for that too.

You cannot cover all the possibilities here, because values are at a more encompassing level than behaviour.
There could be thousands of possible forms of behaviour that could support or undermine your values,
depending on the situation. But you can get an idea of
the sort of actions that support or violate your values.
Then think about the following questions:

Are your rules for your values easy or difficult to meet?
Two possibilities here. First, you have many different
    rules about what breaches your values and few about
    how they are met. Second, you may have only a few
    rules, but be extremely sensitive to your values being
    breached, like a thermostat that has been set too high.
How far are you in control of your rules?
Are they freely chosen?
Does the evidence you look for come predominantly
    from you or from others?

Are there are more ways to violate your values than
ways to meet them? If your values are difficult to
meet, it would be very hard for you to be satisfied,
as you have many more opportunities to feel bad
than to feel good.

Alternatively, are there more ways for your values to be
met than violated? If so, it would be easy to meet
your values and you would have many more opportunities to feel good.

Now you have your values and the corresponding rules that
let you know they have been met, think about your goals.
What do you want? It's your life. Is it leading you anywhere?

Personal Leadership Exercise 3: Your Goals

Take the five areas of your life (personal development,
work, relationships, leisure and health) and write down
the three or four main goals you have for each area.
Have a mixture of long-term goals (10 years or more in
the future), medium-term goals (5–10 years) and short-
term goals (the next 5 years).

Put down exactly what you want in the best of all possible worlds. Do not let your thinking be chained by
what is happening *now*.

How you will know when you have achieved these
goals?

What will happen, what will you be seeing, hearing
and feeling, when you achieve these goals?

Now think about each goal in turn. How far away do
they seem to be? Some may seem quite close. Others
will seem a long way away.

Do you have goals at different distances?

How do you feel about the near goals and the far goals?

How does the distance of the goals affect how
motivated you feel about achieving them?

If some are far away, pull them closer to have a better look at them.

Are you satisfied for the moment with your goal list?

Where do they seem to agree?

Is there any place where they seem to clash?

What do they suggest about the sort of person you are?

What do they suggest about the shape of your life at
　　the moment?

Do you feel that you are moving forward towards what
　　you want?

All goals imply the capability to achieve them. What capabilities will you need to develop to achieve these goals? For example, when I set myself the goal of writing several books, I knew I would have to model good writing, I would have to be more focused in the way I worked and I would have to organize my time better. These capabilities suggested certain tasks (demanded certain tasks, actually).

Leadership is the issue here, so look first at the big picture, not the detailed objectives. Those come later and will spring naturally from the shared vision you will develop with others.

Personal Leadership Exercise 4: Your Vision

Your personal vision is unlikely to appear fully formed in a few moments. Start thinking about the goals you have and the values that matter to you. Let's take your job as an example:

What great things do you want to accomplish that
　　would bring those values together?

When you retire or leave your job, what will you have
　　wanted to achieve?

How will the things you like about your job help you
　　to achieve them?

What would it be like looking back knowing you had achieved these things?

You are wandering on the seashore, digging your toes in the hot sand, thinking of nothing in particular, when you see an ornate bottle of coloured glassy material being washed up by the waves. It has a strange device on the stopper. You stop, rescue it from the water, pull out the stopper and, you've guessed it, a towering genie coalesces from the smoke. What are your three wishes?

The genie says that he cannot grant them immediately, but you will get them eventually. What do you want to accomplish? Quick! The genie is starting to dissolve already...

Organizational Vision

Leadership starts with your personal vision, but the same process applies in organizational leadership. Here you have to create a vision for the organization. It belongs to everyone, but no one exclusively; everyone has to work together to achieve it. Vision is always greater than you can accomplish on your own. It will be inclusive rather than exclusive; it will unite people, not restrict them.

Developing an organizational vision also involves being clear about values, goals and objectives, and also must include a competitive strategy.

Personal vision answers three questions:

What do I want to accomplish?
How do I want to accomplish it?
What is important to me?

Organizational vision must answer some slightly different questions:

What are we trying to accomplish?
What are our values?

How do we deliver results?
How do we cope with change?
How do we get a competitive edge?

Business success demands high performance using distinctive abilities and processes that have value to a defined set of customers. A vision forms a focus for this, an established point for the business to organize itself around.

How do you build a vision in an organization? In four ways: telling, selling, consulting and creating. A leader will use whichever best fits the situation.

Telling

No surprises here. Telling is exactly what you would expect: you tell others the vision and expect them to follow it. 'This is what we will do!' For this you need leadership based firmly on authority and what you say needs to be direct and truthful.

Telling is useful in that it may be the only way out of a crisis. A company in trouble needs a strong top management team and chief executive to lay down a clear pathway to recovery. Generally speaking, the worse the situation, the more likely the company will use the telling way – no time to do anything else and it would be a dereliction of duty for the top management to avoid their responsibility. If the plan goes wrong and leads deeper into the wilderness instead of to the promised land, then top management will be blamed and heads will roll.

Telling needs credibility and authority, however, or it will seem oppressive or paternal. Used too often, it may create resentment and dependence and stifle creativity in the business. Unadulterated telling no longer works as a management style; it's the paternal wing of command and control. It does not create a shared vision, it just creates *a* vision and people will not feel they own it because they have not been consulted.

Usually, telling accompanies the next style – selling.

Selling

Selling is telling plus benefits. Selling is persuasion, you want people to 'buy into' the vision. You sell them the benefits and try to link them with what they value.

As a general management style selling works quite well, but what do you do if people do not buy? Trouble appears when people suspect that the suggested changes will happen whether they buy into them or not, so the whole exercise may look like a sham. Agreement will be more compliant than communal, based on the presupposition that the job of management is to tell people what to do because management knows best. Questionable assumptions.

Selling never carries everyone, but it usually convinces more than telling.

Consulting

Consulting shapes the vision by asking people what they think. It is a flexible means with less control and more trust. It usually involves a cascade approach, using small discussion teams of up to a dozen people. Starting at the top, each of the team members takes the process a step downwards until everyone has had a say. Then all the views are taken back to the top.

How far the vision has been set in concrete before the process starts rolling is important and whether the process actually expands or builds on the vision depends on how receptive the top management will be. The 'Chinese whispers' effect can distort the message – each person changes the message just as little, but by the time it reaches the top again, it can be drastically different from the original version. Also, no one wants to be the bearer of bad news, so the news that reaches the top may be biased in favour of what the board wants to hear.

Consulting still assumes that the vision is created from the top down, but here it trickles down, as opposed to being pushed down in the telling approach and sold down in the selling method.

Creating

This is the most rewarding but also the riskiest way to create a shared vision. Everyone is consulted and no one assumes they know best. When it works, the vision emerges from the total process and represents the whole business.

However, this method does need a business culture where people feel they can really express what they want. In an organization used to a lot of telling and selling, attempts at creating may be met with cynicism and uncertainty. It is a roller-coaster ride, risky because the top management has to give up the idea that they know best. It may seem to lead to anarchy. And when everyone has a voice, they will not agree on everything. Yet this is valuable. Disagreement surfaces assumptions, about the people and the organization, and can lead to a better understanding of both. Unless very carefully handled, however, it can also lead to chaos. Welcome to the challenge and the risk of creating – it comes with no guarantees!

Some organizations venture down this path, but soon think better of it and slide into consulting. It is almost true to say only an organization with some degree of shared vision can use this creating process – you have to have it already to do it. The practice is a powerful one and must have a leader, at least at the beginning, but a vision created this way will be truly shared.

These four approaches – telling, selling, consulting and creating – all have their strengths and weaknesses and there is no right method; leaders use the one that will work best given the situation.

Management Styles

Think of telling, selling, consulting and creating as management and problem-solving styles and how you start a joint project or work with others to solve a problem. What do you do?

- Do you simply tell them how it is going to be?
  This works best if you genuinely know more, if you
  are in the best position to see the future consequences, if the situation is already difficult and if
  you have the personal credibility to make your
  solution stick.
- Do you try to convince them of the benefits?
  This is usually better than just telling, because it
  allows people to connect what you say with what
  they want and to see what the benefits are for them,
  if any. Again, you need personal credibility for this
  to work. (And what do you do if they are not
  convinced?)
- Do you gather all views and then decide?
- Or do you have a free discussion where all voices
  are equal and let the solution emerge without
  knowing in advance exactly what it is going to be?
- Do you use a different style in different situations?
  And if so, how do you decide which style fits the
  best?

It is worth considering all these points because once you
have a vision for your organization, it still has to be elaborated into measurable steps and projects and it has to be put
into action. The more people are involved in creating it, the
more they will own it, feel it is 'theirs' and the more they will
be personally committed to making it work. And a business
will also need to be linked with a competitive strategy or it
will be squeezed out of the market.

When a shared vision does evolve, it must have enough
flexibility, enough ambiguity, for it to continue to fit the
changing organization. The organization that puts the strategy and vision into effect is not the organization that created
the strategy and vision, nor is it the organization that the
strategy and vision was created for. Change is the only constant, so the vision and strategy have to be flexible. But a
workforce motivated and organized by a shared vision is one
of the most powerful competitive advantages possible.

At the beginning of 1997, I was part of a consultancy team that worked with a corporate client on establishing a new vision and direction. This media company had grown up by taking over half a dozen smaller businesses, but had never really formed itself into an integrated unit. It had no overall identity, consequently it consisted of half a dozen fiefdoms, each with its own director, all pulling in different directions. Sometimes they worked with each other, sometimes against each other, but all were concerned about keeping their position. Everyone was good at their job, but their efforts often worked against what other groups were doing. The leaders were not all leading in the same direction. The whole group had just appointed a new managing director and she was determined to get the company into shape. Without a radical restructure, it was clear that it would not last another year.

We spent several days with the leaders of the company and set out to confront limiting ideas and to be honest with each other. Vision setting will not work without honesty, so everyone was encouraged to say what they knew to be true, yet feared to say, within a framework of mutual respect and a shared search for a solution. The directors and top managers worked with us as a group for a number of days to establish a shared vision and the new CEO worked as an ordinary member of the group, with no extra influence, although her presence was a powerful reminder that the group had to change and of her commitment to that process.

There were several ground rules – first, no blame! I have been to meetings where managers start by analysing what is wrong in great detail and this is usually a mistake, like complaining about the airport food and missing your holiday flight. When companies get into trouble there is usually too much internal focus anyway and the only justification for spending more time at it is to find a way of breaking out of that trance. So we began not by raking over what was wrong, but by clarifying the leaders' destination. What did they want? Some parts of the business were doing very well and the directors of those parts needed some convincing that there was a problem at all, though most people were clear about what was wrong. The problem was how to establish a direction to put it right.

The company needed to be innovative in its chosen niche in the media market, but innovation was scarce. There were some innovative individuals, but they felt isolated, as there was no support for an innovative culture, although (paradoxically) innovation was highly valued.

The main difficulty was that there was a low level of collaboration between different parts of the organization. Typically, one company would ask for information or services from another, but communication was poor, messages were unclear and often they did not get what they wanted, so they gave up on the formal channels and a whole informal way of getting things done developed that bypassed the normal management procedures. These informal channels did not work very well either and actually guaranteed that poor communication would continue, because it was not supposed to exist, so was covered up and the underlying problem was never addressed. Everybody just made do the best they could while complaining vociferously. Also, in desperation, companies went outside the group for material and ideas, because they were tired of waiting for them. The company which was supposed to supply these then complained that it was being bypassed. One of our tasks was to convince both companies that they had colluded (unintentionally) in producing a situation that did not suit either.

We set about working systematically to establish a vision, by asking the key questions. First we established some core shared business values: integrity, innovation, openness and commitment to excellence. These are by no means unusual – many businesses have the same core shared values, but they will mean something different to each business because every business will put them into practice a little differently and have different ways of gauging how they measure up to them. We established what evidence we wanted for these values: fewer customer complaints and more joint projects were two of many. Next we discussed the stakeholders in the company – staff, partners, clients, suppliers, investors and shareholders.

The group wrestled with producing a vision statement. Our main work during that time was to stop it from coming to a premature conclusion, as we wanted to keep open to ideas. It is very tempting to go with the first reasonably good idea to be proposed and is much harder to keep searching, knowing that there is limited time, knowing that it is important, yet still waiting for the best to emerge.

Eventually the group's thoughts crystallized around a vision statement. How we reached it was interesting. One of the group headed the advertising department and was acknowledged to be very innovative. We asked her how she came up with ideas. She had a very simple strategy: first define the industry standard and then find a way to go against it. 'That's how to catch people's attention,' she said. This strategy became the idea that sparked the vision statement.

Several goals came from this. The first was to create an atmosphere and environment that fostered innovation. Their actual environment did not help – the building was old, uncomfortable and a tangled mass of computers and wires that had been stitched together over the years. This was a metaphorical picture of how they used to operate! They had already bought another building, however, and were in the throes of moving offices.

The second goal was to develop a greater knowledge and skills base and to ensure that their process and delivery were flawless. The evidence for these goals would come from more joint projects between the companies, a greater volume of ideas, industry awards and public acclaim, better retention of staff, a reduction in absenteeism, fewer customer complaints and a better financial performance. All these goals had to be *measurable*. It is pointless to set less absenteeism, for example, as evidence unless it can be measured. That means there has to be a method in place to measure it and existing figures with which to make a comparison.

The final days of our time together were spent on project management. The objectives were turned into projects, each

one with a sponsor who had responsibility for t
and who would give a progress report to the gr
next meeting. The group also took responsibility
in a way it had not done before. True, the company had ...
back to the wall, but this group had met in previous years,
thrashed over the same sort of problems and then gone back
to their little empires and carried on doing what they had always done, and of course nothing had changed. Now they
could not do this because they were aware of their old dys-
functional patterns and how the system of the business was
working to keep them from changing. No single person
could change it, not even the new CEO, it had to be a team
effort. In business systems, the person who breaks step will
not be able to establish a new way unless enough people follow to give the new system a chance of working. When teams
work together, being honest, trusting each other, being prepared to confront limiting ideas with a shared vision and
having the strength of character to face unpalatable truths,
then great and rewarding changes can happen. Whoever is
at the front of the room facilitating the process, everyone in
the room is a leader.

Bibliography

Nanus, B., *Visionary Leadership*, Jossey-Bass, 1992
Peters, Tom, *Thriving on Chaos*, Alfred A. Knopf, 1992
Quigley, J., *Vision: How Leaders Develop It, Share It and Sustain It*, McGraw-Hill, 1993

4

ON THE ROAD

Motivation

Leadership starts from your vision. That is what motivates you. But what is motivation? Another abstraction. Another of these strange words like 'leadership'! It could be argued that there is no such thing as motivation; it does not exist as an independent quality, but is something we ascribe to people who want to do things. It reminds me of a play written by the seventeenth-century French playwright Molière as a savage satire on the medical opinion of the day. In this play, a panel of highly revered doctors speculates on the reason why opium puts people to sleep. They think about the question carefully and after much learned argument come to the conclusion that opium puts people to sleep because it contains a 'dormitive principle'. In other words, it puts people to sleep because it put people to sleep. A description has become an explanation. Likewise, 'motivation' does not explain anything – just think of it as a useful shorthand for the energy that comes from opening the gap between where you are and where you want to be. You can't measure it, touch it, see it, hear it, smell it or taste it, but you can sense it in people who know what they want and are prepared to go for it. It shows in their voices, you see it in their eyes.

This energy can either come predominantly from without – extrinsic motivation – or from within – intrinsic motivation – and can flow in four different ways:

Aversion

This is 'negative motivation'. It occurs when someone sets a goal you don't like and you react *away* from it. What you are asked to do may violate one of your values, it may be too much hard work for too little return, the disadvantages may outweigh the advantages, or you may simply hate the idea, so you refuse to comply, unless forced. There are several ways of refusal: you can say 'no' openly, or you may say nothing but do nothing either, or you may accept from a misguided sense of responsibility and then sabotage the task – covert refusal.

Being able to say 'no' is very valuable. It defines your boundaries and your values. 'No' sets limits. When we are children, it gives us our first independence, and if you have recently been in the company of a two-year-old, you will know just what I mean. Young children like to say 'no' on principle every so often.

Doing nothing also has power – if you cannot influence events by what you do, then at least you can block them. At any age, refusal sets our boundaries, defines who we are and what we stand for.

There has to be a compelling external reason to overcome aversion, either high reward or very unpleasant consequences. In extreme cases, nothing will work.

An insurance company approached a friend of mine to train some of their direct marketing telephone salespeople. They wanted NLP training to build rapport with customers over the telephone, find out what they wanted and meet objections more effectively. When he met their senior managers in their oak-panelled meeting-room in the City of London to discuss the project further, he found this was only half the story. What they really wanted was to restructure their organization. They were changing the nature of their products and wanted to target more entrepreneurs who ran their own businesses. The insurance sales agents had very little training in this new market segment, let alone telephone rapport skills.

My friend was sure that the company would not get what they wanted from the sort of sales training they were asking him for, so he said that he was unhappy about taking on the training if it was isolated from the wider context and business structure. On its own, he did not think it would address the problems they were facing. It seemed to him they were attempting to make an identity level change with a capability solution. When a business changes its identity it will often need new skills, but these will flow from the change, they will not produce the change. The company said the training was their preferred solution, so they parted company in amicable disagreement.

I think my friend decided for the best. The short-term financial gain was not enough to offset his values about training, or his enlightened self-interest, for if the training did not deliver, then this company would not be a repeat client and his reputation might suffer. So my friend was motivated to avoid the work. The group of values it met (financial, prestigious, enjoyable training) did not counter the values it went against (satisfactory long-term solution).

Most business training gives disappointing results because it is not linked to the larger business context and to real measurable business benefits in the service of a shared vision and values. The trainer should be acting more as a consultant and be involved in the discussion of how the training will be supported in the company and how the results will be measured. Otherwise training is just a change of scenery and will give little or no result. And guess who will get the blame when it fails to deliver? Yet if the trainer is even halfway competent, the failure will not be down to them but be because the training was not clearly linked to the business and supported inside the business. In fact training should be set up so that it is impossible for it not to give results.

Inertia

This is when you don't move at all — you just don't have enough energy. It actually takes more energy to start moving than to keep moving, because it is usually easier to keep on doing what you are doing already than to do something different. As much energy keeps you back as pulls you forward.

So unless you are really motivated, inertia may kick in. This may happen for two reasons. First, you don't care one way or the other; the proposal hasn't set your bells ringing and lights flashing, so it's easier to sit tight. You don't step back, but you do not put your hand up either. Second, you are caught between two values. You have a good reason to move, but also an equally good reason for staying put. Result – nothing happens. But then – horror! You are in a double bind because no choice means no movement and that was one of the two alternatives.

Another friend of mine, who worked for a pharmaceuticals firm in India, got an offer from a firm in Rawalpindi who wanted to hire him as a consultant. They claimed to be affiliated with a United States based consultancy firm, but my friend was not sure exactly what 'affiliated' meant in practice. The contract involved a two-year bond, with four months' initial training, after which they offered him a 25 per cent rise on his present salary. He was torn – safety first or off into the unknown? He found out as much as he could about the new offer, but it was still hard to make up his mind because the choices were so different. How to balance risk against salary? In the end, he fell back on his personal vision – both his present job and the new offer were steps on the way to what he wanted from his professional life. Moving was risky and it did not bring him any closer to where he wanted to go. So he stayed put.

What appears as 'motivation' is not a simple push in one direction. Our actions may take us in one direction, but they are more like the current of a turbulent river – the outcome of many different eddies and cross currents, as well as the hidden rocks and weeds in the river. The current does sweep in one direction but it is the result of all the different forces working for and against each other. Sometimes the cross currents all support the sweep in one direction. Other times the stream meanders along sluggishly or the water stays still and brackish on the top although there may be currents in the deep waiting for the right conditions to come to the surface.

Willingness

Now we are moving. Here a person is willing to do the task either because it is rewarding in its own right or because there is sufficient outside reward to make it worthwhile. The current has stared to flow, perhaps only a trickle, but enough.

Enthusiasm

What we normally call 'motivation' is the space between willingness and enthusiasm. When we are enthusiastic, either the task is very rewarding in its own right or the external rewards are great enough to make it an attractive proposition. The current flows enough to go white-water rafting. In business, when people are enthusiastic about their work, they create a business culture that is a pleasure to work in and it acts as a magnet to attract others. Customers like to deal with people who enjoy their work and companies prosper when everyone works from choice, with passion and energy. This priceless energy cannot be bought.

Unfortunately, you can create aversion and inertia much more easily than willingness and enthusiasm. It is easy. For a start, do not listen to what people want or what is important to them. Or, even worse, make a show of finding out what they want and then ignore it. When employees are asked about what sort of office they want, what sort of structure, how they want to work, they get excited and enthusiastic. When nothing happens or when something completely different is imposed, that is worse than not being asked at all. Why bother?

Another good way to demotivate people is to ignore their achievements and take good work for granted, but immediately comment on the slightest drop in standards. Worse, make these standards of little relevance to their job, but enforce them to the letter. Act as if people are not trustworthy, ask them to account for all their time, question any time away from the work. One telephone sales company I know kept track of all the times the agents were away from their telephone, including the time they spent in the toilet and their tea and coffee breaks.

Being condescending or sarcastic is also very demotivating, as is applying unfair professional standards, for example not giving a sales person a bonus because of a personality clash.

All these actions make for a culture where people do not feel valued and they breed fear, blame and paranoia, all feeding off one another in a downward spiral. This is obviously not the way to lead.

Rewards and Penalties

Leaders tap that energy and passion that come from what matters to people. People will always want to do a task that brings them closer to their vision. Leaders may also offer external rewards to make it worthwhile. In business, this brings us to the perennial key management question, debated in boardrooms ever since people came together: How do you get people to work? Or the more recent, softened form: How do we get people to want to work?

There are three reasons people want to work. One, they are doing a task that matters to them and that they enjoy. Leaders create this whenever possible. Here the energy comes from within – the work has an intrinsic reward regardless of any outside reward offered. Making a workplace fun, challenging and pleasant to work in is worth more than any incentive scheme. *Leadership works as much as possible with values and intrinsic rewards.* Bosses rely on outside pressure. Leaders use values. They may use external rewards, too, but these rewards must fit the values of the people who are working.

A problem with rewards is that both rewards and punishments come from the outside, whereas motivation comes from the inside. Too great an emphasis on rewards and punishments gives the insidious message that the work itself is intrinsically hard and unsatisfying and people have to be tempted, cajoled or threatened to do it at all. Neither the proverbial carrot nor the stick is very satisfactory, but what do you expect of a metaphor that treats people like rabbits or donkeys?

Threatening people with dire consequences if they do not do what they are supposed to do may certainly overcome inertia and refusal. People will work if the consequences of not working are bad enough, but what of the quality of the work? Punishment produces compliance, not results, and certainly not enthusiasm. Nor does it foster creativity. Threats produce anxiety and anxiety hinders the free flow of ideas that creative thinking needs. This reminds me of a car sticker: 'The flogging will continue until morale improves.'

Managers sometimes justify the stick by pointing to better results, with the assumption that the threats caused the improvements. Alas, this is unlikely. One event coming before another does not automatically mean that the first is the cause of the second; the rooster does not make the sun rise every morning, although it may think it does. Bad results are much more likely to improve than get worse due to the simple law of statistics known as regression: results average out over time. Poor performance will eventually improve even when left to itself. The law of regression is not personal, just statistics. It casts doubt equally on better results being caused by rewards. Very good performance falters because it meets limits; leaders have to identify those possible limits in advance and allow for them to consistently shift the average upwards and deliver sustainable improvement. It takes something extra to sustain good (or poor) performance over a long period of time.

The 'carrot' approach is the basis of incentives, bonuses and rewards. It works on the principle that people are motivated by rewards, not threats. Does it work? Certainly. Rewards are good for overcoming apathy and inertia. Do they produce creative work? Not necessarily. People will produce good work for reward, for money, for recognition and for satisfaction. But how well do rewards work as an extra incentive, on top of a fair payment? How well do they work in getting people to work smarter, rather than harder?

Research over the past 25 years has found no evidence that people work more productively or more creatively when they are expecting a reward than when they are rewarded equally, or on the basis of need.[1] Usually it is the other way around: the best people get the most money; that is paid for talent and results, not for motivation. There is no simple relationship between reward and effort.

People are not mechanical and predictable, they change and adapt any system of rewards to their own ends. Also, what starts as an extra bonus soon gets taken for granted and becomes normal, just as we get accustomed to background music. We enjoy it, then we expect it. But we notice when it stops! So rewards can demotivate in the long term unless you keep cranking them up.

Have you heard the story of the eccentric inventor who lived in a tumbledown house on the edge of a village? A group of half a dozen of the local children used to gather around his gate at weekends shouting rude names and laughing. They threw cans into his garden and damaged his wooden fence. One morning the man came out to greet them. 'You don't shout loud enough,' he said, 'and you keep yelling the same names. I'm getting bored. I'll give you a pound each tomorrow if you come and shout the loudest and rudest insults you can think of.'

Of course, the kids thought this was great. They came the next day and shouted some choice insults they had learned especially for the occasion from their older brothers the previous night.

'Not bad,' said the man, 'but that's still rather tame. I'm disappointed in you. Come the day after tomorrow and if you can do better, I'll give you 50 pence each.'

The children came, shouted long and loud, and the man gave them their reward. "That was good!' he said. 'Come again on Saturday but I can only afford 10 pence.'

'Only 10 pence!' sneered the children. 'No way!'

So they stayed away.

And never came back – it wasn't worth it.

As well as causing problems of escalation, rewards can undermine teamwork if they are given to individuals. There is a delicate balance between teamwork and individual work, and giving individual rewards is not the best way of getting the best work out of teams, as it goes against their whole ethos. One study carried out at 20 American social security offices found that the introduction of an individual merit pay had no effect on office performance, even though it was carefully linked to key performance indicators such as the accuracy of processing claims and time taken to settle claims.[2]

Merit rewards for team members can be even more problematic. These 'co-opetition' teams rely on competition between members to give the best overall result. Sales teams are an example. Only one of the team will get the coveted 'salesperson of the month', with its large bonus, and this can breed bad feeling. Bad feeling can also arise where departments are given bonuses based on performance and one person's mistake loses the reward for the whole department.

With many organizations moving to a way of working based on cross-functional teams, team performance is a major business issue. Leadership fits perfectly into creating high-performing cross-functional teams. It is not the opposite of teamworking, but complementary. Leaders bring teams together, and in a good team, everyone can be a leader, as they work together. Any one of the team can take over a leadership function, depending on the situation. The best teams are all made up from people who have developed themselves as leaders.

Many companies embrace teams in practice, but have a pay structure that reinforces individual striving at the expense of the team. Quantum, the computer hardware manufacturer in California, shows its commitment to teamwork by putting all its employees, CEO, managers and hourly workers on the same bonus plan that is linked to overall return on capital.

Back to rewards – and a reward is only a reward if it is valued by the recipient. Obvious perhaps, but I have seen many examples where management has offered incentives that no one wants. A reward is what you want, not necessarily what you get. Money is one type of reward, but not the only one, and it tends to be overused.[3] Everyone deserves a fair financial reward and good salaries should be paid, but paying money to try to get people to work faster or smarter does not usually work well.

What is the right reward? It depends on who is being rewarded. It may be money – the all-purpose reward, valueless in itself, but capable of being converted into most things that people value. Some things, however, it will not buy – respect, reputation and a fun atmosphere, to name three. If you have to try and buy these, it shows you don't have them.

Money is not just a reward in an organization – it goes to maintain the system and to encourage work that the organization values. Show me where the money flows and I will show you what an organization really values, regardless of what it says it values. Money is a means of control as well as a means of reward. It has strange and often contradictory effects on people. For example, those people who demand money because they feel hard done by or have not had a salary rise for some time will often leave the organization even (or especially) if the rise is given. Why? I guess it wasn't really money they wanted. They wanted something else, perhaps challenge, more recognition, a better environment. They didn't get it, they got money, and nothing else changed.

Many surveys have shown people rank money as the third or fourth value in their working life. Yet the same surveys show that when asked what they thought was the most important motivation for *others*, people gave money as the first choice. Strange that we think others should want what we do not want.

To assume that people will work for money is to assume that they are completely rational, everything else is equal and they are out to get the most money they can. Many people work far harder than they need to earn their money, because they enjoy what they do. They choose a poorly paid profession but they are happy in it, or they choose an employer who pays lower wages because they like the people, the atmosphere and the culture that goes with the job. I like the story of Tandem computer, a firm recently acquired by Compaq. If you went to them for a job, they would not tell you the exact salary that went with it, only that the rate was competitive for the industry at the time. They reckoned that if you came for the money then you would leave for money as well and they were more concerned about building a culture than attracting people on the basis of salary. I would propose that any company that thinks it can motivate and retain staff purely through individual monetary incentive is not paying nearly enough attention to its environment, values and culture. Ideally, you want prospective employees to choose you over your competition who are offering an equal salary package.

I know many people who passed up promotion to continue working with people they like and trust. We all invest time and effort in activities that pay us nothing, 'just' because we enjoy them. This is no justification for paying people poorly or less than they are worth, but it casts doubt on purely financial incentives and bonuses. So, if we do not use money as a reward, what shall we use instead?

Leadership is about inspiring people through a shared set of values. Think back to your most satisfying, most creative work. Why did you do it? How did you do it? Something made it important and worthwhile – something you value highly. Just as your values motivate you, so the way to motivate others is through their values. So to be a leader, you need to know what matters to your companions. The odds are they will share some values with you anyway, but to find out more, you need to ask questions like:

What's important to you about this?
What do you value about this?
Why is this important to you?
What does that get for you that you value?

You may not be used to asking personal questions like this. Maybe no one has ever asked you those sort of questions.

Normally we tend to assume what matters to us is also important to others, or at least assume their co-operation or indifference. When we assume other people have the same values and value equivalents we do, we give them what we need (but they may not), while getting from others what they like (but we may not).

Whenever I think I know what others want, or what they value, I remember a story told me by my daughter's primary school teacher. She had set an essay for the whole class with the title: 'The most exciting thing that ever happened to me'. The next week, she collected their work in and enjoyed reading it. She planned to read the best stories to the whole class. All the stories caught her imagination until she came to the story by Tony, one of the quietest boys in the class. He had written, 'I went to America and found some treasure in the desert. Then I got lost. Then my parents found me and I went home.' That was all. The teacher was intrigued. The next day, she took Tony aside and said, 'Tony, I was reading your story last night and it sounded really exciting, but I don't really know what happened. Can you tell me a bit more?'

Tony told her of how he went to America on holiday, and how he and his family went to the Arizona desert and visited an archaeological dig. The excavators had allowed Tony to share their discoveries, including some Native American pottery, and then he had become separated from his parents in the desert. He had nearly died.

The teacher sat on the edge of her seat as the story unfolded. 'Why didn't you write all this?' she asked.

'Thought you would work it out,' he said. 'It's only details.'

Tony had a marvellously complex tale in his mind and because it was so real to him, he thought it would be equally real to others. He assumed others would know or be able to work it out. He will learn, I hope, that the good things of life are in the details.

Once you know what is important to others, then you need to find their rules, their value equivalents. How do they know when their values are being honoured? How do they know when their values are being violated? The best rewards are value equivalents and they will be different for each person.

For example, your companion wants to be recognized for their contribution. You might ask a question like, 'How do you know when you are recognized?'

They might reply, 'I'll be praised and my work will be publicly acknowledged.'

Then you could ask, 'What lets you know when you are not recognized? What would happen or what has happened in the past?'

They might say, 'I did good work and my boss took the credit.'

So, for that person, public acknowledgement is important, but being praised in private is not enough.

I witnessed one such argument, where a supervisor maintained he did recognize his colleague's work ('But I told you it was good!') and she maintained he did not ('You never told anyone else, no one else knows!') Unless the rules for the value are brought into the open, both parties can retire to their corners feeling aggrieved. When you know about value equivalents you can avoid those pointless arguments that settle into a 'Yes, I did' 'No, you didn't' holding pattern that just circles round and never gets satisfactorily resolved.

When you have asked these value questions a few times you will never again assume you know what people value or how they decide they have got it. The questions are personal, but rightly so – they treat each person as an individual, with their own wishes, hopes and goals. You may be surprised how quickly people will tell you what matters to them when you are genuinely interested. They are often delighted that someone has taken the trouble to ask. Occasionally, they will regard you with suspicion, wondering if you have an ulterior motive, or they may expect to have to justify what they say. But never ask people to justify their values. Like everything else that affects us deeply, they are not logical. They are not illogical either – logic is irrelevant.

George Bernard Shaw wrote, 'Reasonable men adapt themselves to the world. Unreasonable men adapt the world to themselves. That's why all progress depends on unreasonable men.' I think leaders adapt themselves *and* the world to advance their vision.

Values and Integrity

A decade of research with over 15,000 managers[4] showed that they look for integrity in a leader above all else. Integrity? Another abstraction, but then values usually are. What does it mean?

The word comes from the Latin *integras*, meaning 'wholeness'. The word 'integer', meaning a whole number, comes from the same root. The opposite is 'disintegration' – falling apart. So integrity means acting as a whole. No double standards, no saying one thing and doing another. Integrity creates trust and trust means being true to your principles. You trust someone you can rely on. Businesses often recite the mantra that they place the greatest value on their people, but what happens when profits fall? Too often the people are the first to go. What do they think of the company then? And, more importantly, how do the survivors feel? Valued? Disenchanted? Worried about who'll be next?

An extensive study of business decisions in medium-sized European companies showed that nearly two thirds of major decisions were taken in line with declared company strategy. That's not a bad score by any means. However only one third of the decisions of middling importance and a tiny one in 20 minor decisions were taken in line with company declared strategy. Well, at least they were true to their principles when it mattered. But this is only from an outsider's point of view. Think what it looked like from the inside. The major decisions, those that were taken in line with company strategy, were infrequent, usually taken behind closed doors by a small group of top people and often kept secret for good commercial reasons that were not generally known. The small day-to-day decisions that affected the employees immediately were frequent and open, but few of them were based on the principles that they were supposed to be implementing. Every day these people saw evidence that the companies were not walking their talk. Who could blame them for becoming cynical? From a leader's point of view all decisions matter, *especially* the small ones.

Here is a quote from Jack Welch, CEO of the American firm General Electric. Welch was generally acknowledged as a strong, capable and unsentimental business leader. He acquired the nickname of 'Neutron Jack' from his efforts to reduce the workforce and get rid of under-performing subsidiary businesses – the buildings were still there but there was hardly anybody left in them. He is quoted as saying, 'Trust is enormously powerful in a corporation. People won't do their best unless they believe they will be treated fairly – that there's no cronyism and everybody has a real shot.' And a further quote: 'If you are not thinking all the time about making every person more valuable, you don't have a chance. What's the alternative? Wasted minds? Uninvolved people?'[5]

When Welch speaks of making people valuable I would translate that as making people feel *valued*. You do this by finding out and acting on what is important to them. Being value focused does not mean being soft or easy or non-competitive, but gives you strength to fight, to compete, to be tough and clear about decisions, because you can trace them back to what is important to you and the people you work with.

Sometimes it seems that what we cannot count does not exist and values and purpose are not easily quantifiable. We have not yet evolved a way to measure them easily. But we can measure their effects in the hardest currency of all – money. What do you think would be the asking price for Microsoft? (Always assuming there is any organization or country on the planet that could afford to make an offer.) It would be billions of dollars. What would the buyer be paying for? Certainly more than the Redmond Buildings in Washington State and Bill Gates' smile. They would be buying a company capable of generating huge profits because of the way the expertise, intellectual capital and imagination of its people have been harnessed. Buildings are easily measured. Human imagination is not, but is worth far more.

In 1988 Philip Morris bought Kraft for close to 13 billion dollars. The hard assets, that is the buildings, offices, warehouses and real estate, were valued at about one and a half billion dollars. The soft assets, the values, marketing ability, brand equity and creativity were worth nearly seven times the hard assets. The same pattern applies to any company takeover. The ratio of a company's stock market value to the replacement value of its physical assets is known as the Tobin ratio, after the Yale economics Laureate James Tobin. Some typical ratios were calculated by *Fortune* magazine in 1991 and they ranged from eight to one for some software companies to two to one for hardware companies with more physical stock. Shared values and purpose lead to competitive advantage.

If an organization is not guided by shared values, layers of management are needed to control the organization. Which of the well-known multinational organizations of the world do you think has the fewest layers of management? You might guess it would have to be one based around values and you would be right. It's the Roman Catholic Church. The Pope is at the top and after him come only cardinals and bishops. Three layers. A community of faith by definition, the Church has little need of a large management hierarchy.

Now which well-known multinational organization do you think had the most layers of management? It would need to be an organization where command and control were important, and where there was little trust. The answer: the Russian Communist party. Springing from suspicion and mistrust, it perpetuated suspicion and mistrust. It was a formidable hierarchy for stifling liberty and free ideas for over 50 years.

Politics and religion are two of the most emotive subjects (perhaps because they are so closely allied with the other two, money and death), so it is perhaps fitting that they hold the records in these fraught areas.

Signposts to the Future

Through offering the promise of making our values real, leaders offer one way for us to dream, to go beyond our imitations, to be part of creating something larger than ourselves, to accomplish something important through and with others as part of a team on a small scale, or as part of a community on a large scale. Leaders point the way past environment, through actions and skills, powered by values and beliefs, past what we can accomplish as individuals.

For example, you cannot build a monument on your own, it takes many people working together. We look at Stonehenge and marvel at the time and dedication that went into positioning those standing stones, and wonder at the vision that drove those architects to create the site. Stonehenge is the memorial of a vision whose breadth we can only guess. I wonder whether any memorial of ours will still be standing in 2,000 years' time for our descendants to admire and wonder how we did it with our primitive technology?

I read that NASA hopes to put the first man on Mars before the year 2008. The round trip will take up to two years. It is the riskiest space mission yet and I wouldn't personally rate it high on my list of holiday destinations, but there is no shortage of volunteers. Leaders leave a legacy, something unique for people to recall. They are remembered by people whose lives they changed.

Every time we push the boundary on the outside world we also push the boundary on our inner world. We open a larger 'idea space'. Every advance in science, art and technology means we have gone beyond the limiting ideas that have stopped us advancing in the past.

I like to collect predictions that turned out to be completely wrong. It is easy to look back with hindsight and laugh at the *naïveté* of our predecessors – historical progress seems inevitable or incredible, depending on whether you view it from the past or the future. I keep the list to remind myself not to be complacent about what is possible and not to look into the future and see only a reflection of the past.

Every invention, every advance in science and art begins with a subversive thought.

Through a Glass Darkly...

Here are some quotes that the speakers wished they hadn't said. Plenty of others shared their opinions as well. How many editorials and pronouncements will come back to haunt our present experts in 10 years' time? I've started my collection already.

'Who the hell wants to hear actors talk?'
H. Warner, Warner Brothers, 1927

'The abdomen, the chest and the brain will forever be shut from the intrusion of the wise and humane surgeon.'
Sir John Ericksen, Surgeon Extraordinary to Queen Victoria, 1873

'Louis Pasteur's theory of germs is ridiculous fiction.'
Pierre Pachet, Professor of Physiology at Toulouse, 1872

'Everything that can be invented has been invented.'
Commissioner of the US Office of Patents, 1899

'Stocks have reached what looks like a permanently high plateau.'
Irving Fisher, Professor of Economics, Yale University, 1929

'Professor Goddard does not know the relation between action and reaction and the need to have something better than a vacuum against which to react. He seems to lack the basic knowledge ladled out daily in high schools.'
New York Times editorial about Robert Goddard's revolutionary work on rockets, 1921

'Heavier than air flying machines are impossible.'
Lord Kelvin, President of the Royal Society, 1895

> 'The telephone has too many shortcomings to be seriously considered as a means of communication. The device is inherently of no value to us.'
>
> Western Union internal memo, 1876
>
> 'I think there is a world market for maybe five computers.'
>
> Thomas Watson, Chairman of IBM, 1943
>
> And finally...
>
> 'We don't like their sound and guitar music is on the way out.'
>
> Decca Recording Company, rejecting the Beatles in 1962

Reluctance

So far we have talked about motivating others, but what about your own motivation? Becoming a leader means changing and change is both a promise and a threat. Whatever your present circumstances, at least they are familiar and habitual. Habit acts like the force of gravity, stopping you from floating away. Our habits are the personal equivalents of those organizational procedures that keep a company running. They are designed to produce the same result consistently with minimum effort. They are extremely valuable parts of an organizational system, until it wants to change, and then they become its enemies.

It would be unusual if, at some point on your journey, you did not feel reluctance. Reluctance lives in that no-man's-land between inertia and willingness, where flesh and spirit are both weak and willing at the same time. We want the stability of what we have, but also the promise of what we want. Reluctance speaks for all those habits that we have built up, so honour that reluctance, it is important. It has a positive intention – to protect you from possible harm and to conserve those things that are important to you about your present situation. Reluctance is the steward of the psyche.

Organizational resistance has the same intention. Organizations have many procedures to achieve consistent stable results. They also tend to recruit those people who fit best with the management culture, thereby perpetuating and strengthening the particular culture and way of working. When an organization starts to change, many people resist, of course. This resistance should be honoured as the other side of the stability that has allowed the organization to be successful in the past.

We form habits as a way of dealing with uncertainty. Uncertainty itself comes from the constant change in the world. We need a measure of stability in our lives, our psychological balance depends on it, just as our life depends on keeping a stable internal environment in our bodies with constant body temperature, fluid balance, breathing, nervous activity and heartbeat. When we find something that works, it makes sense to keep doing it.

In our bodies we have homeostatic systems to literally dampen down any change that becomes too uncomfortable. When we become too hot, we sweat, more blood flows to the skin, so we lose more heat. The more we sweat, the more heat we lose and the more we cool down. So, the hotter we get, the more we compensate. This is called homeostasis, which means 'keeping the same state'.

We have similar systems in our personal lives that keep us in balance. We have a pre-set 'comfort level' but, unlike the fluid level, *we can influence it directly*. The greater the gap between our desired comfort level and our actual level, the more disturbed we feel. The greater the gap, the more we try to damp down the disturbance until we are back inside our comfort zone. Change can, of course, bring about a huge difference between our desired comfort level and our actual level.

How can we use this? First look on reluctance as the friend that warns you of change. Secondly, remember that your social life has far fewer restraints than your physiology. Our circumstances do change, so trying to stay exactly the same in the face of continuous change would be not only foolish, but also impossible. We have to keep the *relationship* between our environment and ourselves constant, but we do not have to keep our lives the same. In fact we always have to change in order to stay the same, just as our skin renews itself every day in order to keep us alive.

When you decide to make changes, as long as the change is in accordance with your vision and values, it will take you to a higher level. Leadership is one example of this sort of 'generative change'. You can deal with the accompanying reluctance by making sure you keep some important parts of your life stable.

For example, last year a friend of mine moved house, remarried and started a new job. He wanted all these changes, but he felt anxious just the same. So he decided that three parts of his life were going to stay the same: his exercise programme, his visits to his children by his first marriage and his work position (he had also been offered a promotion). He said that he felt these were the counterweights he needed to balance the other changes. He thought of it just like a set of scales. He needed a counterweight to keep his life from tipping up.

Similarly, the body's homeostatic mechanisms work a little like a central heating thermostat. With a thermostat, you set the temperature level in advance to what suits you. When the temperature drops below that level, the thermostat makes the heating come on. When the heating goes on, the temperature rises, bringing the thermostat up to the set point. Think about your response to change in the same sort of way. Where have you set the level on your change thermostat? How wide a comfort zone do you have? How much change can you tolerate comfortably before you try to stop it? If you have a low tolerance, then you will respond to even the slightest change with reluctance. If you have a very high tolerance, then your life may be quite the opposite – there may be so much change you may live in an atmosphere of personal chaos where it is difficult to hang on to anything for very long. Life with you will be very exciting, if perhaps exhausting. So use reluctance as a signal not only to look at the changes you are making, but also to question where you have set your level. Sometimes we leave the level stuck on a childhood setting and do not think to adjust it.

Think what would happen if a thermostat were programmed to respond to temperature changes of a tenth of a degree. It would be switching the heating on and off every few minutes. A change thermostat set too sensitively would mean you would be constantly making plans and then dropping them, responding to every slight shift – you would try to micromanage your personal life, and be sensitive and intolerant to anything out of the ordinary.

On the other hand, imagine a thermostat calibrated in five-degree units. You would get quite cold before the heating came on. A personal change thermostat set like this would mean you would stay the same for long periods and then suddenly realize and change drastically. Somewhere between the two extremes lies a range that allows us to live well and adapt. (I suspect that to handle modern life we need to have a wider band of tolerance than people had in the past.)

Your Personal Change Thermostat

Does your life seems to be full of changes, or have
    very little change?
How do you react to change?
How wide a tolerance do you have for change?
Think of some changes that you have made that
    worked out well. What was good about them?
Now think of some changes you made that did not
    work out well. What made them unsatisfactory?

Think of the changes you would be making in becoming more of a leader in your life and work. What
    has stopped you making these changes before?
Has anything changed since then?

What might stop you on your quest to develop yourself as a leader? On the outside you may find your relationships changing – you may lose friends, though you will gain friends. You may even damage your career prospects if you are presently working in a company run on command and control lines. No good deed goes unpunished in these sorts of organizations! You will also have to overcome weaknesses in yourself and to develop new resources, just like a hero in a story. Overcoming these weaknesses is the main step in becoming a leader. How might you keep the advantages of your present situation and still develop yourself as a leader?

In general, the fear of change comes in two flavours:

1 The understandable fear of success – new problems, new challenges, no old certainties. I think our schooldays also make us wary of success. Success in a school examination brings the reward of – being eligible to take another, even harder examination! When are the examinations really over? Only when you decide they are.
2 Success puts your head above the parapet. You become a target for the envy of those less successful than you. So you need to plan for success just as you need to plan against failure.

These are real dangers that you need to think about. The other fear, of course, equally understandable, is the fear of failure. Failure may be something that you are already painfully familiar with.

Turning Past Failure into Present Success

You may have tried to make changes in the past and been unsuccessful. So they seem even less attractive now. Perhaps that was not the right time, but the old memory still has an effect. Now you can heal the memory.

Think back to the time when you tried to make a change that failed. See yourself at the time. What were you trying to achieve?

Watch yourself as if on a movie screen. Be completely detached from your screen self, as if it's not really you, but a friend who is role-playing to show you what happened and in a moment will ask for your advice. Watch the movie through to the end.

What can you learn from the incident so that it will not happen again in the same way?

What would you have liked to happen instead?

With the benefit of hindsight, what advice would you give the person in the movie that would help them make the situation better?

Imagine yourself doing that now, reliving the incident in your imagination, seeing yourself acting differently, and see how the situation resolves itself in a different way. Then blank your mental screen.

Do this at least three times and blank your mental screen after each action replay.

Now step into the picture. Imagine yourself back in the situation. Go through it again, in the new way that you have just tried out. Take your own advice – act differently in the situation and see how it turns out now.

Is this satisfactory?

If not, then go back to watching the original movie and seeing what else you can learn and what other advice you can give. Then step into the situation again and act that new advice. Do this until the situation turns out to your satisfaction.

There is one other possibility. The change may not have been tried at the right time. Whatever you did then, it may *never* have turned out as planned.

In this case, think what circumstances would have to have changed in order to have made a difference in that situation.

Have those circumstances changed in the meantime?

If they have not, what can you do to influence them so that you can make this change safely now?

You can also use this technique when you have a difficult decision to make. Imagine your future self as a guide who has made the change successfully. What advice would they give you?

The Dark Side of Change

Change is risky, so you need to do some downside planning. Downside planning means covering yourself in case of disaster – a process that makes insurance companies very rich indeed. But when you have possible disaster covered and you know that even if the worst comes to the worst, you will be alright, it is much easier to go ahead.

As you look ahead to your proposed changes, what are the dangers? What could go wrong? Just because something is worth doing, there is no guarantee it will be successful. Motivational tapes and literature exhort you to 'Be positive!', but optimism and faith alone are no substitute for careful planning. Put the three together, however, and you have a good chance of success.

When my daughter was 11, she enrolled at a local youth centre for a canoeing course on the Thames. She could swim, but the Thames is wide, fast flowing, brown and uninviting. She came back from her first lesson quite indignant. 'I thought canoeing was about staying out of the water,' she said. 'They taught us how to capsize for half this lesson!'

I was *very* glad. This coach didn't say, 'Capsize? Don't even think about it! Think positive!'

Once you know how to deal with disaster, you don't need to think about it. This is why riders are taught how to fall off horses and racing-car drivers are taught what to do in a crash as part of their basic training. If you have no plan to deal with disaster, the thought of it may haunt you, and with good reason.

Exploring Reluctance

Think of the change you plan to make and ask yourself these questions:

What other important changes could this bring?

What is important about not making the change?

What will I lose by making the change?

What will I gain?

What do I want to stay the same in my life to balance this change?

How important is this change to my development as a leader?

How important is it to develop as a leader?

What is the greatest external difficulty I would face in developing as a leader?

What is the biggest internal weakness I would face? (This is also your greatest asset. Overcoming this will be the quickest way to leadership.)

What quality would I have to develop the most to combat that weakness?

What relationship do I see between the external difficulty and the internal weakness?

Here are four questions to focus your mind on downside planning and its opposite, upside planning:

What is the worst that could happen if I do not succeed? (And am I covered for it?)

What is the best that could happen if I don't succeed? (And how attractive is that?)

What is the worst that could happen if I do succeed? (And am I prepared?)

What's the best that could happen if I do succeed? (And is that really OK?)

Remember leadership has a dark side too. People will expect you to be special, they will project their hopes and fears onto you and then expect you to resolve them. If you refuse, they may become indignant. The greater public exposure you have, the more likely this is to happen, as people will relate not to you but to their fantasy of you. Public acclaim is wonderful – as long as you live up to what the public wants. Leaders may be expected to be perfect, that is, to embody the ideal of perfection in other people's minds, and this can be a great burden.

Cultures vary as to how much humanity they will tolerate in their leaders, though leadership is a risk in any culture. It does set you apart from others, although your shared vision and goals will keep you in touch with them. Leaders do need to be an example, but idealizing leaders soon turns to idolizing leaders. No one is perfect and the higher the pedestal you stand on, the more visible your feet of clay.

Be careful of the expectations of others, but be careful of your own expectations too. Leaders have to be realistic. When you know yourself better, however, you will know more about leadership, and as you develop as a leader you will in turn know yourself better.

Vision is important, but I have met too many steely-eyed visionaries labouring under the tyranny of a personal vision or mission which blinds them to the simple pleasures of life. They are like the Ancient Mariner in Coleridge's poem, always buttonholing you to tell you about their mission when you want to get on with what you are doing. They are addicted to their vision, seem to suffer withdrawal symptoms if they spend a day away from it and have a driven quality that is exhausting to be with. I think vision should be part of your life, not life part of your vision. It is something that should bring you closer to others and not alienate them. Vision is like a light that lets you see the possibilities of a fuller life. You may focus it into a powerful torch beam, or it may be like a softer daylight that allows you to see your way more clearly. Acting from a vision does not mean that you cannot laugh, have fun or relax.

One last story, told to me by my Bulgarian friend Christo Georgiev. Vassil Levski is a national hero of Bulgaria. Born in 1837 in Karlovo, he was martyred during the revolution that freed Bulgaria from the Turkish rule of the Ottoman

Empire.[6] He was a remarkable leader by all accounts, a professional revolutionary who had little previous fighting experience yet in the space of two years created an underground movement made up of over 200 committees in towns and villages throughout Bulgaria. It was a kind of state within a state, with its own police force, postal services, official archives and, remarkably, audited accounts. Although Levski has been romanticized by his countrymen, he seemed to have all the leadership qualities – a vision of a free country shared by his fellow countrymen, the ability to inspire others in dangerous circumstances, and a great grasp of strategy and tactics in battle. Levski was against Turkish rule, but he also built up a community of resistance fighters. The Christian Church was his ally and monasteries used to hide him, often in specially built secret caches. He was killed in 1873 and the Turkish rule of Bulgaria was overthrown in 1877.

He is reputed to have said, 'If I win, I win for the whole people. If I lose, I lose only for myself.'

References

1 See Morton Deutsch, *Distributive Justice: A Social-psychological Perspective*, Yale University Press, 1985, and Kenneth McGraw, 'The detrimental effects of reward on performance' in M. Lepper and D. Greene (eds), *The Hidden Costs of Rewards*, Earlbaum, 1978, and, for a good summary of the evidence, Alfie Kohn, *Punished by Rewards*, Houghton Mifflin, 1993.

   See also Crystal Graef, *The Overcompensation of American Executives*, Norton, 1992. This book exposes how top executives are rewarded whatever their success (or lack of it) in a company.

2 See John Pearce, William Stevenson and James Perry, 'Managerial compensation based on organizational performance', *Academy of Management Journal*, June 1985

3 See Jeffrey Pfeffer, 'Six dangerous myths about pay', *Harvard Business Review*, May–June 1998, for an excellent discussion of the place of pay incentives in business.
4 James Kouzes and Barry Posner, *Credibility*, Jossey-Bass, 1993, pp.12–15
5 Quoted in Noel Tichy and Stratford Sherman, *Control Your Own Destiny or Someone Else Will*, Doubleday, 1993
6 See Marcia McDermott, *The Apostle of Freedom*, Allen and Unwin, 1967

GUIDES AND RULES OF THE ROAD

Journeys can be dangerous and the best laid plans can go wrong. What will you be packing to help you on your way? What sort of survival kit does a leader need? You cannot take much, you want to travel light (but not too light) – a bulging suitcase will only slow you down. What resources do you need to help you?

On your journey there will be challenges that you will meet with three kinds of resources to match the three attributes of a leader:

1 You will need *self-skills* – to develop yourself so you can lead by example and develop your vision.
2 You will need *relational skills* to influence and persuade others to accompany you, to develop others as leaders and build excellent teams.
3 You will need *strategic thinking skills* to understand the situation so that you can take a long-term view rather than make a short-term fix.

Mentors

Your greatest resource is a person you can trust and who is willing to guide you. If they have made the journey themselves, then so much the better. A mentor is such a person. In the Greek epic poem the *Odyssey*, written in the ninth century BC, Mentor was the old friend and counsellor of the hero Ulysses, and tutor to his son Telemachus. From here, the name has found its way into our language as a trusted friend and teacher. Mentor was inspired by the Greek gods, and the English word 'enthusiasm' has its roots in the Greek words meaning 'to be possessed by a god'. Enthusiasm can be such a strong force and inspiration that it seems to come from the gods. A mentor is an enthusiastic friend, a coach, someone to confide in, a shoulder to lean on. No one, certainly no leader, is invulnerable and self-sufficient.

Who has been your mentor in the past? A mentor does not have to be an old grizzled man with a flowing white beard, looking like a Hollywood depiction of the Old Testament God. Anyone can be a mentor. A real person makes the best mentor, but a mentor does not have to be a person. You may have a book as a mentor. Nearly everyone remembers a book or a series of books that had a great effect on them when they were children. Perhaps they even shaped what they wanted to do in life. Every good story has a mentor character, some written so well that they seem to spring off the page and speak directly to us. A mentor may be a character in a film. In the *Star Wars* trilogy, Obi Wan Kenobi, the Jedi knight, becomes the first mentor to Luke Skywalker. Even when Obi Wan dies, he still acts as a mentor. Later on, Luke is mentored by Yoda, who was Obi Wan's mentor. Yoda hardly fits Luke's vision of a Jedi knight, which makes the point that mentors are not always what we expect them to be.

You can choose your mentors and sometimes your mentors choose you. I count my children as mentors. I have learned a tremendous amount from them, although I did not always appreciate the lessons at the time.

While writing this book I read a newspaper article about the joys and perils of being a stepfather. The writer took the cyborg character played by Arnold Schwartzenegger in the film *Terminator 2* as a role model for a good stepfather (at least in part) – not for his indestructibility, but because the erstwhile terminator is as unswerving in protecting the young boy in his care as he was unyielding in his homicidal pursuit in the first film. A cyborg programmed to kill is not the obvious choice of a role model for a stepfather, but part of his character was perfect. Mentors never provide a *complete* answer or role model – do not copy a mentor, but help them bring out the best in you, so you become more yourself. As long as you carefully select what parts you model, many fictional or historical characters can act as a mentor. How about the absolute unswerving motivation and dedication shown by the Tim Robbins character in the film *The Shawshank Redemption*? Or the inventive zeal of Harrison Ford as Indiana Jones in *Raiders of the Lost Ark*? They used these qualities in their quest, and you can take them and use them in yours.

In many cultures there is a rich tradition of animal guides. Animals show qualities more starkly than we do, undiluted by intellectual considerations or worries about long-term consequences or morality. They cannot speak, so their behaviour speaks for them. Whenever I go to the zoo, I like to watch the big cats prowl their cage. They seem to have a tremendous solidity and at the same time an incredible lightness and grace. They seem to be able to balance relaxation with instant action when needed. We think cats are lazy, but it seems to me they only do what is necessary and use the minimum amount of effort to do it. That is a quality I would like.

A place can also be a mentor. There are places where you feel comfortable, places that suit you, places where you can think. Natural beauty has an effect that is inspiring and soothing at the same time, and that always takes me back to the beauty and tranquillity of the sun setting behind the island of Molokai, looking out from Maui in the Hawaiian islands. At sunset it goes very quiet, the air grows denser and softer and seems to absorb sounds, and they disappear into it, leaving no trace. However frantic life becomes in London, I can relive that moment. There are such mentor places everywhere and once you find them, they are always available because you can carry them with you.

Choosing your Mentors

Choose a real person, someone you can trust, someone with whom you can talk over your ideas, perhaps a member of your family, a friend or a work colleague.

Now choose three other mentors for your journey. These mentors can be people you know, people you have heard of but never met, historical or fictional characters, animals, or places that inspire you. Mentor is an honoured and honourable status, so choose well. You have to trust your mentors.

1 The first mentor should be one who would help you with the greatest external difficulty you are likely to face *(you will have identified this in the 'Exploring Reluctance' exercise, p. 96).*
   Who do you know who has overcome those sort of odds or would be able to overcome them?
2 The second should be one you feel can help you with the greatest internal weakness that might stop you developing as a leader *(again, see 'Exploring Reluctance', p. 96).* Do you know someone who has overcome this weakness or could help you overcome it? Choose a fictional character if you do not know any suitable real person.
3 The third mentor is a free choice. Who do you want to make up your panel of advisers? Perhaps someone very different, to balance the others?

In medieval times, English kings and lords had a court jester or fool. He would tell jokes, play tricks and ostensibly keep everyone amused. He was allowed to step outside the bounds of normal polite words and behaviour, poking fun at people, reminding them of their weaknesses, deflating their egos when they became too full of their own position. He was a special sort of mentor to the lord of the castle. Because of his unusual position he was allowed to say things that other people could not get away with without punishment. He gave the outsider's view, the slightly skewed view, ironic, quirky and critical. There are some wonderful examples of this in Shakespeare's *King Lear*, where the fool is the only person who will speak the truth to the deranged king and the only one who stands by him in his madness to his tragic end. Indeed, the king acts more foolishly than the fool does. A court jester is a great mentor.

Have at least three internal mentors, the more different, the better. As a leader, you will not face easy problems with a fixed answer. If you did, you wouldn't need a mentor – a mathematician or a logician would be good enough.

When you want advice, take a few minutes for yourself alone and conjure up an image of each mentor. Make them as vivid, colourful and 'real' as possible. Ask each mentor in turn for their advice. Take your time. You may get nothing at first, you may get something obvious or you may get something unexpected. You may get no answer at all, or a direct or indirect one, or one without words. Your answers may come in the form of stories, pictures, sounds, cryptic allusions, obscure references. They may appear like dream fragments. They may even be tasks. Whatever they are, they are answers, not necessarily the 'right' answers, but maybe better ways of looking at the question.

The sort of problems you face are not going to be easy cut-and-dried problems, but more like complex shapes in a dark room. You do not know what they are and you find out by lighting them from different angles to see their true size and shape. Mentors help you, and the more different the mentors, the more diverse and illuminating the viewpoints. Three similar mentors would all light up the same part of the problem and you would get an excellent understanding of that part, but the rest would be as dark as ever.

When you have your responses, think about the following questions:

What do they have in common?
How are they different?

What actions do they suggest?

Outside mentors are not your only resources. Take a few moments to list all the resources you have. Group them into these areas:

People
There are many people who can help without being elevated to mentor level – friends, work colleagues, family and acquaintances. Some people will be helpful in certain situations, while mentors are helpful in any situation.

Role Models
Who do you know who has gone through the same sort of challenges as you?
What did they do?
How did they think?

You can take these people as models for ways of thinking as well as action.

Physical Environment
There are many possibilities here – where you live, all your possessions, books, magazines, tapes, computers and computer software as well as the resources of your neighbourhood can all help you. In fact your whole environment can be a resource.

Skills and Personal Qualities
You can group these into three types:

Self-skills – your personal qualities, those qualities you like about yourself and those qualities others like about you. Also, think about some qualities that other people have criticized. How could these be an advantage? For example, if people say you are over-critical, then you have a fine eye for detail. Stubborn – you don't quit easily. Any quality that is a disadvantage in one situation

is a resource in another. Just be choosier about where
you apply it.

Relational skills – the skills you have for dealing with others.

Problem-solving skills – what sort of problems can you solve?
What games are you good at? How could you transfer
some of the successful strategies in those games to 'real'
life?

Values and Beliefs

What is important to you? Does this give you passion? What
beliefs do you have about yourself and others that can help
you?

Your values and beliefs are very powerful resources.

Unpacking Skills

Sometimes we keep skills in boxes and do not apply them
where they are needed. Often we do have the communication skills we need, but not where we need them, so we
think we do not have them. I remember a woman who
talked to me about her problems at work. She was very
short-tempered in meetings and would try to push her plans
forward and convince others she was right. Afterwards she
regretted the scene that ensued and whether she won or lost
the argument, it did not advance her career. I asked her
what she was good at and enjoyed doing. She admitted
sheepishly that she was good at counselling her friends
when they were in trouble. Here she asked a lot of questions, found out their point of view and got a lot of
satisfaction from helping them and from coming up with
creative solutions that they had not thought of. She was constantly keeping track of how they felt by their voice tone,
gestures and what they said.

In the work situation, she said she just told the other
people what she thought and told them they were wrong.
Her goal was to convince them that her point of view
was right and she only knew she was succeeding when they

conceded the point, as she did not pay attention to any on-going feedback at all. She saw the other people as her opponents.

I wrote down these points and we looked them over from a detached point of view. She could not believe she acted so differently in the different situations. She decided to treat the work situation as if it were a counselling situation. In other words, she looked on the people she was arguing with as her friends. This did not mean she had to like them, only that she wanted them to feel good about talking to her. She paid attention to their feedback, using their voice tone and their body language to guide what she said next. She asked more questions instead of telling them what to do. The results were immediate – there was a better atmosphere at work and her discussions were more constructive. Then she took her 'telling' mode and switched it to other situations in her work where she needed to be more assertive.

You can switch your resources round too.

Switching Resources

Pick a situation in your life where you are not getting the result that you want – maybe in a work situation, maybe dealing with others or with a particular person. Think about a typical instance and then answer these questions:

What are you trying to achieve here?

How do you judge that you are getting what you want?
    What signs do you pay attention to?

What do you do to get what you want? Make a list of all the actions you take and the sort of things you say.

How do you view the other person in the situation?

When you have done that, think of a situation where you did get what you wanted. This can be any situation. It does not have to be with the same person or with an-other person at all. Then answer the same questions:

What do you want?

What do you pay attention to to know that you are getting it?

What do you do to get your goal?

If there is another person in the situation, how do you view them? If there is not, what attitude do you take?

Now put the two sets of answers side by side and look at the differences.

Typically, in the unsatisfactory situation, people find that they have only one goal, that they do not track the feedback they get, but only know that they have got it when they have got it. This is useless as evidence. Imagine a salesperson who only knew that they would make the sale when the customer said, 'Yes.' They would have no feedback on how to communicate their product. A good salesperson reads the customer all the time – voice tone, body language and words – for buying signs. When one approach does not work, they try another, and the only reason they know what works is because they are paying attention all the time.

Finally, in the first situation, you will only have a few actions that you take, with no fall-back plan if they do not work, and the other person will be seen as an opponent, someone standing in your way. You probably feel bad about the situation and this does not help. It means that each time you meet this person the bad feeling hovers in the background, and also the worse you feel, the less resourceful and inventive you are likely to be.

In contrast, where you are effective, you will have multiple goals, have many options to get them, be tracking the situation all the time and have a positive attitude towards the task.

How could you switch the skills that you have when you are effective to deal with the unsatisfactory situation?

What extra goals could you get out of it?

What signs can you pay attention to the whole time, not just at the end?

How many different ways can you think of to get what you want in that situation?

How can you think about the other person in a positive way? You do not have to like them or even be friendly – you could view them as a teacher (you are learning how to be more effective) or as a worthy adversary (like a competitor in a sport).

After deciding your answers to these questions, imagine acting this way at your next meeting with that person. See the meeting through in your mind's eye. Better? More comfortable? If not, generate some more options. Make sure that they fit with your values. Sometimes when I have done this process with businesspeople they discover that actually they do not want to do business with this other person at all and they can get what they want in another way.

Finally think about your response in the first situation. Is there a place in your life where that would be useful?

This whole exercise is at the heart of good communication with others. Your influencing skills as a leader are based on your goals and vision, your ability to read the feedback from others and the amount of choice you have in what to do.

Influencing Others

Be clear about your goals in the situation. Have three at least.
Make sure they are connected to your vision.
Pay attention all the time to what the other person says, how
they are saying it and their body language. Your sensitivity
is your only guide to getting what you want.
Have many choices of what you can do.
Find a way to look on the other person in a positive way,
even if only as someone who can teach you patience.
Be clear that the whole situation meets your values and
ethics.

A leader needs determination. Not the gritted teeth, stiff upper lip and bulging veins in the forehead type of determination – all wasted effort. You need the patience and concentration of a Samurai swordsman – still, centred, prepared to circle their opponent waiting for the right time to strike – or the balanced relaxation of a cat.

I believe we all experience this sort of determination, usually in childhood, when we have to master many complex skills that adults take for granted. They leave us to our own devices in the name of 'character building' or they want to help, but we refuse their advice because we really want to figure it out for ourselves. For example, when I was four, I liked solving jigsaw puzzles. My grandparents gave me a particularly complex one that Christmas. It showed the battle of Waterloo, although I did not know or care what battle it was. It showed Napoleon, resplendent in his scarlet and gold uniform, with what looked like a black, folded paper boat balancing on the top of his head, desperately gesticulating at his retreating troops. (The puzzle was obviously made in England and not in France.) Horses, canons and foot soldiers milled around him in the smoke. I liked the picture, it captured a kind of heroic despair that appealed to me. I don't remember how many pieces this puzzle had, certainly more pieces than I could comfortably count. This jigsaw kept me busy for days. I got the edges without much trouble. Edges are easy, but after that I got stuck. My parents, grandparents and uncle all offered to help me. Once my grandfather took up a piece and told me where it went. He even went to put it in for me. I said, 'No! I want to do it myself!' and took the piece out again and defiantly mixed it up with the others. The more I got stuck, the more determined I became to complete the puzzle. I was not going to let small pieces of painted cardboard get the better of me. Eventually I finished it after what seemed like months (actually four days). I still remember that ferocious determination and I see it in other children. Children are supposed to have a short attention span, but it has the focus of a laser beam. Maybe it doesn't last long because it is so intense.

There was probably something you wanted to master when you were young. It may not seem like much now, but at the time it was important. Gandhi is reputed to have said, 'What you need to do may not seem very important, but it is vitally important that you do it.' That is the quality a leader needs.

Leaders and Losers

Leaders tend to think of themselves as winners. They are optimists and this comes from a belief that they can and will influence what happens. They start with the idea that they will succeed unless something stops them. They prepare as far as possible to avoid problems, looking out for all the possible pitfalls and solving them before they happen. They focus on results – not with naïve Pollyanna-like hope that all will be well regardless, but with a determination to succeed and an expectation of it. Winning is a belief and a state of mind. The winning result comes from the winning state of mind. Losers, on the other hand, tend to start from the idea that they probably won't succeed.

How is it possible to believe you will achieve your goals? Sometimes the odds against you seem too great. But whatever misgivings leaders have, they act *as if* they will achieve their goals. No one knows the future, but acting as if you will succeed gives you the best chance, and is just as realistic as pessimism, given that you have prepared as best you can. In the absence of certainty, optimism is not such a bad idea.

The Winning State of Mind

The winning state of mind is a skill. You can develop it yourself by changing the way you create your expectations.

How do we create expectations? In three ways. First, we do not give every experience equal attention and importance, but *delete* most of it. At every moment there are thousands of possible things we could pay attention to. We cannot take them all in, so we develop rules, mostly in childhood, about what we pay attention to.

What are you aware of right now?

And what were you not aware of that you could have been aware of?

We all see the world differently. Fifty people looking on the same scene will give 50 different accounts of it. We filter our experience through our memories, values, interests and preoccupations, always keeping an 'emergency channel' open for danger signals like the smell of smoke or the threat of violence. And we do not remember what we have not noticed.

Think of it like choosing what television channel to tune into. Sports, current affairs, soaps, action films, news and documentaries all vie for attention. We cannot watch them all at once, so we watch what interests us. All the channels are available all the time, but you cannot watch them all at once.

Secondly, we *distort* and change our sense experience, reading meanings into situations that may not be there or were not intended. This is the basis of suspicion and paranoia, but also of creativity. Life would be very boring if everything had one 'right' meaning.

We also *generalize* from our experience. We make rules about the world, based on the past. Then we apply those rules to new experiences. This is a really essential skill, otherwise we would have to work out every problem from scratch every time. All numbers can be added and subtracted in the same way. Drive one car and you can drive any car like it. Use a key in one lock and you can open any similar door. Generalizations are habits of thought. They make the world safer, less ambiguous, more predictable. But generalizations can be limiting when we learn the wrong lesson or try to shape the future in the image of the past. We get stuck when we always try to explain our present experience by our past experience. You can tell you are generalizing when you hear yourself say words like 'all', every', 'none', 'nobody'.

Beliefs are generalizations about the past projected onto the present and future to shape it in the image of the past. Generalizations and their associated beliefs work best with inanimate objects – things that do not change much. People, on the other hand, do change. One person is not like another and the same person may change drastically as a result of some powerful experience or simply as they grow older. Generalizations need updating.

When we generalize from incomplete or unrepresentative experience, we form mental models that make the wrong predictions, but because beliefs act as self-fulfilling prophecies it is hard to find out, because we are less open to counter examples. A few years ago, I worked with a junior manager in a paper company. He has two assistants but was loath to delegate work, particularly anything important. As a consequence, he was always overworked and his assistants were underworked. He did not see how he had arranged it like this and he complained bitterly. Several of his assistants had quit because they did not feel challenged and valued in their job. When they quit, it reinforced the manager's view that the assistants were poor quality, so he was quite right not to delegate. Why did he not delegate? He used to, but a couple of large projects he had turned over to his assistants had turned out badly. He told me that he then decided that 'delegation wasn't working', an interesting ambiguity in meaning, and kept all the important work to himself. 'If you want something done well,' he would say, 'you have to do it yourself.' He was determined, as he put it, 'not to make the same mistake again'. I told him he was avoiding the wrong mistake. Delegating was not the mistake. His mistake was not finding out what went wrong those times he did delegate, so that he could avoid those circumstances in future. His brand new mistake was to treat all his assistants as if they were the one who botched those past projects. That particular assistant had moved on, but my friend had not.

This has everything to do with optimism because optimists generalize in a certain way. First, they think of bad experiences as a combination of their action, plus an unfortunate set of outside circumstances that were beyond their control. They were not totally responsible, though they may take responsibility for the results. They use the results as feedback, analyse them to find out where they went wrong and work out what to do differently next time. So they learn from the mistake in a very specific way. They also take the result on the neurological level of behaviour. It was something they *did*, but it does not make them a incompetent *person*.

Secondly, they treat the experience as an specific incident that will have little effect, if any, on their other activities.

Thirdly they see it as an isolated incident that does not set any precedents. It will not always be that way.

When they do well, they reverse that way of thinking: they put more emphasis on their action and give themselves credit for timing it right. They take credit for what they did and feel good about it. They link it with all the other occasions when they did well and look forward to further future success. They take it to an *identity* level. They feel a competent and successful person, because they did these things well. Optimists pay attention to different parts of their experiences.

Optimism is not luck, or a sunny disposition, but a strategy of how you think about your experiences – a winner's strategy. The loser's strategy on the other hand is physically unhealthy. It is known in medical literature as ISG (Internal, Stable, Global). *Internal* because it focuses on what you did and leads to self-blame. *Stable* because the pattern of failure looks unchangeable and *global* because failure colours all areas of life.

This ISG loser's pattern was studied over 35 years using a group of healthy and successful members of Harvard University classes from 1942 to 1944. They were tested to see whether they tended to use the pessimism strategy (ISG) or whether they were more optimistic. Every five years the groups had a thorough medical examination. As they got older, their health tended to worsen, but the gap between the healthiest and the least healthy got larger as time went by. Overall, men who used the optimistic strategy at age 25 were healthier later in life. The health of the pessimistic group showed a marked deterioration, especially between the ages of 40 to 45, that could not be explained by any other variable. Statistically, the link was as robust as the one between cigarette smoking and lung cancer. Surprisingly, we do not put the same effort into teaching children to generalize optimistically as we do into persuading them not to smoke cigarettes. Pessimism should carry a health warning.

Leader's Strategy:
Turning Mistakes into Knowledge

A bad experience is:
a result of their actions and outside circumstances.
feedback to learn from so that it does not happen again.
the result of a mistake. It does not make them an
    incompetent person.
a specific and isolated incident.

A good experience is:
evidence of good judgement and timing.
something to take credit for and feel good about.
something to learn from and duplicate.
proof that they are a competent person.
the latest in a pattern of success.

Loser's Strategy –
Turning Mistakes into Disasters

A bad experience is:
the result of what they did. They are to blame.
something that shows they are an incompetent person.
something that will affect many areas of their life.
the latest in a catalogue of disasters.

A good experience is:
proof that they were lucky this time.
the result of what they did, not who they are.
an isolated incident.

Balancing Task and Relationship

The Journal of European Quality published an interesting series of articles about European business leaders in 1997.[1] They identified eight leadership styles by asking the employees (regarded as the leader's 'internal customers') what qualities they thought were most important in business leaders and built up a profile of an excellent leader in European business. Eight leadership styles emerged as the most important: the team builder, the captain, the strategic, the creative, the leader focused on task, the involved, the specialist and the impulsive. The survey showed that the most important style was the strategic. Strategic skills were most valued – setting a long-term direction, setting a competitive strategy and guiding the business through the market opportunities. Second was the task-focused leader, then, close together in third place, the captain (leading from the front by commanding the respect and trust of the employees) and the team builder.

Setting the vision is the first part of the leader's work. The second part is setting the strategy, goals and tasks that are necessary for the vision to be achieved. The third part is to make sure these tasks are done, otherwise no one reaches the goals or realizes the vision.

Once leaders have set strategy, they face the challenge of balancing the demands of the tasks to be done with creating good relationships between themselves and their team members. The two are compatible: the focus on the task is important, but does not mean relationships have to be neglected.

Getting the balance right between task and relationship can be tricky. Tasks need to be done, but people are not robots, they have emotions, expectations and values. Creating a good relationship is part of getting tasks well done. Tasks may be boring and meaningless unless they are seen as steps in the pursuit of goals and a vision that the workers value. Leaders need to motivate people to want to do the task, to appeal to their values to get it done.

However, the more ill-defined the task, the more important the relationships between people. Think of some times when you were in a situation where you were not sure what you were doing. The more uncertainty, the more you depend on support from others. The more competent and confident you feel about the task, the less you need that support. Support builds confidence.

So, to get tasks done well, you do need to focus on relationships. In extreme circumstances, say mountaineering, a team needs to trust that each member of the team can do the task and – just as important – will do it. They count on each other. The more dangerous the situation, the more important the immediate task, and the most important it is that the team members trust each other. Teams without good relationships at the start may fall apart under task pressure.

I know a manager who works in the customer service department of a furniture dealer's. Jenny specializes in getting teams into shape. She is very good when they are untrained and reluctant to learn the ropes. She focuses on the task. People who like her say she has a strong directive style, people who don't say she's 'bossy'. She tells people exactly what to do and when, where and with whom to do it. She gets the job done, then builds relationships. She's also good with teams that are willing but untrained. Again she focuses on the work, but in a more relaxed way, because she knows they will not take advantage.

Alan works for another division of the same company. He is good at building relationships. He is especially good with capable but under-performing teams – they know what to do and they can do it well when they want to, but they may be a little burned out. Alan isn't directive, he gives them lots of support and usually manages to coax the teams away from the fire. Jenny and Alan are outstanding in their different ways.

One ill-fated day the company swapped them round. Jenny took Alan's teams and Alan took Jenny's, and the result was a disaster. My work in that company was to model the skills of each so Jenny could learn how Alan builds relationships and Alan could learn how to be more task-oriented when necessary. They would both gain as leaders, as they would be able to switch between the two styles – task focus and relationship focus – depending on the situation. No leader is so good that they cannot learn more, and Jenny and Alan were intrigued that the two sorts of teams were so different.

It was interesting to find out what Jenny saw as her skills and how the teams saw her. She thought she was better at building relationships, but the teams and other managers she worked with thought she was better at getting the job done. People respected her, but felt little warmth for her personally. Alan knew he was easy-going and people liked him, but if a job turned out badly, he didn't know how to toughen his approach without appearing harsh.

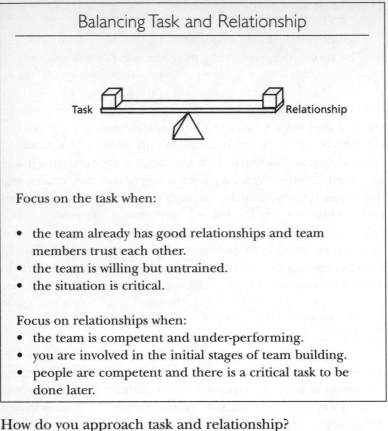

Balancing Task and Relationship

Focus on the task when:

- the team already has good relationships and team members trust each other.
- the team is willing but untrained.
- the situation is critical.

Focus on relationships when:
- the team is competent and under-performing.
- you are involved in the initial stages of team building.
- people are competent and there is a critical task to be done later.

How do you approach task and relationship?

When you work together with friends or colleagues do you focus more on the tasks to be done, or the relationship you have or need to build?

Do you alter the balance of task and relationship depending on what has to be done in the different circumstances, or do you keep the same balance in all your activities?

The Rules of the Road

Corruptissima republicae, plurimae leges.
(The more corrupt the republic, the more laws multiply.)
Tacitus, Roman historian, AD 55–117

Relationships come down in the end to trust. Trust is based on common values, and also on understanding and sharing boundaries about what is allowed and what is not allowed. What defines boundaries? Boundaries are the edge of the permissible, they separate, they give structure and define the space you have to play in. Shared rules give shared boundaries. There are both formal and informal rules in any organization and no group, whether it is a team, family, community or gathering of friends, can exist without them, because rules are codified common understanding. When you break shared rules, you forfeit trust.

Roman Law and Common Law

Boundaries can be set in two very different ways, one known as Roman law or Napoleonic Law, the other as common law. Roman law prohibits what it does not allow. So unless something is explicitly allowed, then it is prohibited. Common law permits what it does not prohibit. So you are free to act unless there is an explicit rule saying you cannot.

Imagine a space available for your ideas and actions. This is your idea space. Where are the boundaries? Roman law puts you within narrow boundaries. Common law frees you to make your own boundaries.

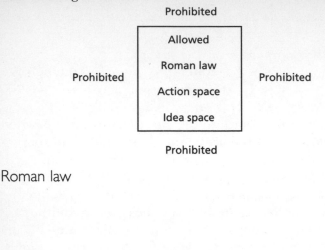

Roman law

Common law

Once your vision and goals have been defined, you have to choose how they are accomplished. Roman law defines the means in a much narrower fashion than common law. It is far less flexible, because it limits choice. No set of rules can possibly be broad enough to cover every eventuality. Roman law tries to specify the means to the end rather than the end itself, and rules proliferate in the absence of shared values and trust. Leaders set the goals but should be as flexible as possible about the means to those ends. Means have to be governed by shared values – the more rules, the less space for values. Rules should not take up value space. The more rules, the less trust, and the less trust, the more rules.

Ends and Means

Leaders set the end purpose, values guide the means to the end.

Vision divides into purpose (destination) and values.

Possibilities rather than necessities set the vision.

Common law sets the boundaries.

Purpose divides into a number of goals.

Goals are divided into objectives.

The objectives are the smaller goals each with a definite evidence for completion.

Objectives are achieved through specific tasks.

Tasks are the work necessary to achieve the objectives and are agreed among the group.

Common law defines how those tasks may be carried out.

Values govern the direction and means to achieve the objectives and therefore the goals, objectives and tasks.

Values

Present state ———————————————— Desired state

So, Roman law stifles innovation, because it restricts the available idea space. Behind it lie fixed principles and an unchanging worldview: this is the way the world is – and, by implication, this is the way it is going to stay. Roman law is set up as the received wisdom to be passed from generation to generation by the appointed keepers of that wisdom. Wisdom may be handed down, but it will be mixed with a large helping of the prejudices, limitations and limiting generalizations of the previous generations. Roman law accumulates, like a rolling stone tablet it gathers more laws, and they are seldom repealed, being amended, elaborated and supplemented until the statute book groans under their weight. Roman law organizations and Roman law countries (the distinction applies all the way up to nations) have a huge body of laws that is being added to constantly. (For example, the French Napoleonic Code never deleted a law, only added new ones. The legacy of Roman law still affects France, which has more laws per capita than any other nation.)

Leadership is a risk in any culture, because leaders by definition move away from the status quo, but hardest in cultures under Roman law. Roman law encourages administrators to enforce the laws. Leaders thrive in conditions of ambiguity and uncertainty, and Roman law cultures and organizations do not tolerate these conditions gladly. A Roman law organization will be more oriented towards discovering errors than exploring possibilities. It will also be more turned towards the past than the future.

Common law is based more on practice and precedents: a living code, modified in the present in order to cope better with the future. Because it permits what it does not forbid, it is influenced by feedback in a way that Roman law is not. Common law can close loopholes when it becomes clear that a practice hurts the community; that still leaves large areas of freedom. Innovations are not against the rules, so people can experiment without fear. Roman law forbids what it does not permit, so innovations are against the rules and may be stopped immediately before any benefit becomes apparent. They have to be justified before they can be approved. It is much easier to see and fix what is wrong than justify something as right. So Roman law tends to add ever more restrictions and relax very few.

A good example of Roman law in action was England in the 1970s when trade unions would 'work to rule' as a bargaining counter for more wages or better conditions. Historically, trade unions arose in the face of management repression to represent working people's rights against the owners and managers of companies. Originally, owners had great power over their employees, wages were poor, conditions were bad and individuals had no chance when they complained and no bargaining power. The unions did not trust the management and vice versa, their roots were in economic and class conflict. The trade union rule book was drawn up to curb the power of the bosses. It laid down in great detail what was permitted and what was not because trade unions members thought (often with good reason) that management would take advantage of any slack or ambiguity. Years passed, business changed, and unions and management formed more of a partnership, but the Roman law of the union rule book was never updated. Consequently, when unions worked to rule, they worked to a labyrinthine Roman law that laid down exactly how things were to be done (or how things used to be done, but were not any more because those methods were too antiquated). Existing practice was governed by common law, new technology, increased trust, shifts in power and new government legislation. It was task based, not rule based. So, working to rule nearly always put a stranglehold on an industry.

Applying the Law

The boundaries you set yourself or others set for you define the space you have for innovation and action. Roman law and common law govern how boundaries are set.

In your work:

Which predominates, Roman or common law?

Does your organization have many rules that lay down only what you can do (Roman law) or does it have rules that say what you cannot do (common law)?

Are the rules open to feedback and do they change as the company changes?

Are there unrealistic rules that have given rise to informal working practices?

How easy is it to get new ideas considered?

Do you have the experience of constantly bumping against the boundaries of what is permissible?

Is there an organizational rulebook?

How often is it changed?
Is it open to feedback?

In your personal life, when you are not sure what to do, do you tend to ask yourself, 'Am I allowed to do that?' or do you ask yourself, 'Is that forbidden?' The first question comes from Roman law, the second from common law.

Instead of saying to yourself, 'I can't do that,' ask yourself, 'Why can't I do that?'

Roman law	Common law
Prohibits what it does not allow	Allows what it does not prohibit
Practice constrained by rules	Rules constrained by practice
Stifles innovation	Encourages innovation
Sets boundaries on your freedom	Sets boundaries on your constraints
Encourages administrators	Encourages leaders
Discourages trust	Encourages trust
Sets the means to achieve goals	Sets the goals – the means are open
Looks to the past to validate action	Looks to the present and future
Not open to current practice	Open to feedback from current feedback
Needs informal practice to be workable	What you see is what you get
Increasing number of rules and amendments to rules	Rules change, the number of rules is fairly constant

Learning

'Education makes a people easy to lead, but difficult to
drive; easy to govern, but impossible to enslave.'
Lord Brougham, 1778–1868, when Lord Chancellor of England

I like this quote, but I would replace 'education' with 'learning'. It makes it more personal and immediate, and separate
from schooling. Learning is how we become leaders and
how we develop others as leaders. How does it happen?

Learning is another sort of journey towards greater skill in
order to get better results. We start with some purpose in
mind – to gain promotion, to finish a project, to understand
ourselves better, to solve a problem or to improve a skill.
When we start, a gap exists between what we know and what
we want or need to know. Learning crosses that gap – once
on the other side, we know it, we have evidence of success.
So we plan, decide and act to get what we want. We get
results (not always what we wanted) and constantly evaluate
whether the results have brought us any nearer our goal. If
they do, we do more of them. If they do not, we do less of
them (if we have any sense) or try something different.
Learning forms a circle like a wheel that transports us towards our goal.

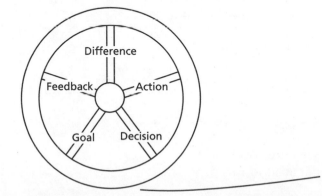

Simple Learning

Simple learning is when learning takes place within existing beliefs, ideas and assumptions. Your results do not make you question your beliefs about the nature of the problem or the sort of person you are. It can all happen within the frame of Roman law.

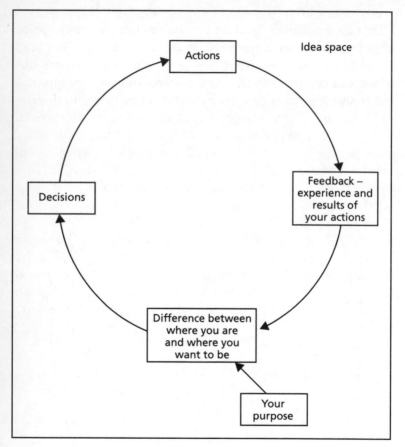

In simple learning, you ask questions like:

How can we solve this problem?
How can we get around this problem?

If you repeat the same action with the same mediocre result, then you have not learned from the previous experience, so you stay where you were. Do not pass GO, do not collect £200. This learning cycle is also known as single loop learning.[2] In practice, when Roman law limits the range of choices and we get stuck, we often break the rules.

Generative Learning

Generative learning is when you question your assumptions about yourself and what is possible in the situation. This is possible with common law, because you have a larger idea space and you can use the results of your actions to question the basis of the problem. Your beliefs come into the loop.

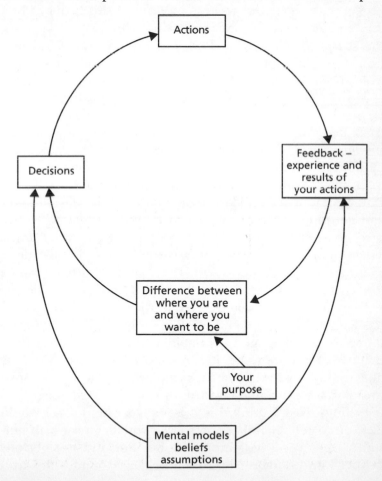

Roman law permits only simple learning – problem-solving within fixed boundaries of thought and action. Common law permits generative learning – learning that has the possibility of not only solving a problem, but also of *eliminating the thinking that caused the problem in the first place.*

Generative learning can build you a faster set of wheels to make the journey – or you may find it would be better to travel somewhere else entirely.

I know a manager in a small department of a media company that deals with advanced graphics software. Phil was very innovative and always looking for improvements, 'If it ain't broke, make it better' was his motto and this brought him into conflict with his manager David, who was not keen on the stream of ideas from Phil. His position was 'If it ain't broke, leave it alone.' He did not want Phil to mess about with any products until they had been evaluated. Phil excelled in getting down to the details of the software, while David was more interested in the bigger picture. Phil felt very frustrated. He did not feel valued in the company and he thought David was blocking his ideas and his chance of promotion. He wanted a chance to prove himself and his ideas.

Phil kept coming to David with new ideas and each time David put him off. Phil knew some NLP and he started to try and get rapport with David by matching general body posture in meetings and also matching speed of voice tone. They got on much better, but David still blocked Phil's ideas. Phil had long arguments with David and tried to convince him that his ideas were worth looking at, but got nowhere.

Phil was a more visual thinker, thinking in pictures. David was a kinesthetic thinker, he relied on his feelings and intuitions. So Phil changed his habitual visual language ('I see this as really important, it can expand our horizons, why does everything have to be black and white?') when he spoke to David. He explained his ideas in kinesthetic language, saying things like, 'I think this is a really strong idea, I would like you to get a handle on it, so that you feel it is worth pursuing.' Again rapport improved, but Phil did not get any further with his ideas. He tried to get agreement with David at a higher level – the good of the company. He said he appreciated David's intention of caution and seeing how the software sold, but he also had the good of the company at heart in a different way. David agreed, but didn't change.

Becoming increasingly desperate, Phil tried to go over David's head to a senior management level, but that did not turn out at all well. David found out and relations deteriorated. David then started passing some of Phil's ideas to a friend in another department. His friend presented them to his manager, who was much more open to innovation, but politics did not allow Phil to take the credit, so his friend's department flourished and Phil became increasingly unhappy.

All Phil's actions were attempts to solve the problem in single loop learning. He was not in a Roman law organization, but David effectively held him in a Roman law trap. He still felt boxed in.

Any of these strategies might have worked, but when they did not, Phil started to question some of his assumptions. Could he be wrong? Were his ideas any good? They seemed to be well received when put forward in another department. Was he hitting his head against a brick wall? Phil was a very determined person and that determination was his greatest resource in coming up with new ideas for products – he would never give up until he could tweak something to improve the software. Giving up seemed like a failure of what he stood for. More thought brought him to the conclusion that his greatest strength in the area of software redesign was what was keeping him from moving on. Determination had shifted to stubbornness while he wasn't looking. There are few if any good qualities that cannot be a liability in the wrong context. Push a quality too far and it turns sour.

Phil applied to transfer to another department. No luck. Finally, he reluctantly resigned and joined another company where his innovative talents were more highly valued. So there was a happy ending, not before considerable wasted effort. But you do not know an effort is wasted until you have tried it, and usually you have to go around the single loop learning circuit a few times before you shift to the double loop pattern and question your assumptions.

Solutions and Resolutions

Leaders face complex problems and need to be able to find their way forward. Some problems are relatively simple – there will be a definite number of appropriate solutions and a clear procedure for solving them. Plotting a route by car, for example, is a simple problem. Also, the more you study a simple problem, the more the possible answers tend to converge on one optimal solution. Complex problems are the opposite. The more you study them, the more possible solutions there seem to be, and more depends on your assumptions about the problem than the problem itself. How can our business stay competitive in the market? What is leadership and how can we get it? These are complex problems. All the important and interesting problems are complex ones. And the assumptions you bring form part of the problem.

Problems can be dealt with in at least four different ways:

1 They can be solved. This is only appropriate for simple problems. There is a single optimal solution, usually in the form of 'What shall we do: A or B?' For example, buy a new car or take a holiday? You solve the problem by doing one or the other.
2 They can be re-solved. Then you see them as part of a larger, wider-ranging problem. Instead of thinking about whether to have a car or a holiday, you shift your attention to earning more money so you can have both if you want.
3 They can be dis-solved. Then they do not matter any more – something more important happens, a sudden illness means you have to use up your savings, so you do not get either, or you win the lottery and can have 10 of both and still have plenty of money left over, or you decide you don't care and stop thinking about it.

4 They can be ab-solved. Then they are not your problem any more. You hand them on to someone else or someone else takes them off your shoulders.

This reminds me of the joke about the man who had borrowed a lot of money from his next-door neighbour and the time was fast approaching when he had to pay him back. With one day left to raise the money, he was frantic, but it was impossible, he would not be able to pay. He went to bed the night before the fateful day and tossed and turned but could not get to sleep, he was too preoccupied. Eventually he picked up the telephone and dialled his neighbour's number. The man answered.

'Hello,' said the first man. 'You know that money I owe you that's due tomorrow?'

'Yes,' came the guarded reply.

'Well, I can't pay you yet.'

And he put the telephone down.

Breathing a sigh of relief, he said to himself, 'OK, now *he* can worry about it instead.'

Leaders need to question their own beliefs and assumptions when faced with complex problems – that means they question all constraints, challenge all assumptions and question the definition of the problem.

Leaders are always asking questions like:

Is this a problem at all?

What are we assuming about this problem?

How else could I think about this?

What else could this mean?

How else could this be used?

Under what circumstances would this cease to be a problem?

What else has to be true for this to be a problem?

What are we doing to create this problem?

Organizational Learning

Organizational learning is slightly different from individual learning. How can organizations learn apart from the people within them? Organizational learning seems to emerge as something greater than and different from the individual learning that makes it up; it seems to arise through the complex interactions of the people together. People know more in a group than the sum of their knowledge, because a sum is addition and learning is multiplication.

A learning organization is a useful shorthand for an organization that constantly changes and experiments using the feedback of its results to change its form and processes in ways that make it more competitive and more successful.

Organizational learning is like a rainbow – something different and unexpected that emerges when all the elements are in the right place. When people in an organization are themselves learning and they are put in a challenging situation, then you have organizational learning.

Knowledge and Information

Organizations prosper depending on how well the people work together to use the knowledge they have. There are far more combinations of water droplets and light that do not make rainbows than that do, and there are far more ways that organizations can fail than succeed.

We often talk of knowledge but knowledge is built up slowly from many sources. Business is inundated with data. Lots of facts all clamour for attention and people must sort through them for *information* – relevant data that make a difference to the business. They extract this information from the overwhelming amount of facts, opinions and analyses that are present in the market.

Business goals set up the filters that turn data into information. They create order from chaos. So the information is only as good as the goals and values that the organization has created. Then this information is co-ordinated and connected, again guided by organizational goals and values. This creates knowledge.

The quality of relationships, connections and communication within the organization allows information to be turned into knowledge. A has information about company X. B has information about company Y. Only if they talk can they see how the market is moving. Then their organization can move with it. There are so many possible combinations that a computer can never create these kinds of insights:

Client information is converted into client relationships.
Production information is converted into production
  innovation.
Market information is converted into commercial
  awareness.

The knowledge you get is as good as the internal networks you have. Knowledge creates value. It helps the organization succeed. Knowledge gives foresight – the ability to look into the future and to see patterns and make predictions. It also gives insight – the ability to see how the present connects with patterns in the past, and therefore which patterns to continue and which patterns to change.

Organizational learning also means the constant creating and use of knowledge to compete successfully. When organizations act on this knowledge, then customers provide feedback and the process starts again. The inherent knowledge within the organization helps to form the filters that extract information from data, so the whole process makes a self-reinforcing circle.

Knowledge management is far more than finding a good computer system to store and manipulate the data. It is about creating networks so people can turn information into knowledge. It is also about valuing and rewarding the people who have part of the intellectual capital of the organization between their ears. Knowledge management must also deal with a system of rewards that makes it worthwhile for people to connect and create knowledge that benefits the organization.

You cannot store knowledge, because it is created all the time in response to the changing conditions. Computers can only store knowledge about past conditions, which may be useful, but is no substitute for intelligent people. Nor can knowledge be treated as separate from the people who have it. A computer is much easier to look after than a person. When a person feels off colour or overworked, they will not be able to be creative. Knowledge management is about looking after and inspiring people. Leaders do this too.

Organizational Learning: Making the Rainbow

People extract information from data.

Data are all the possible facts, analyses and opinions.

Information is data relevant to the business. The more you know about the business, the better filters you have.

Knowledge comes from connecting information to create value, insight and foresight.

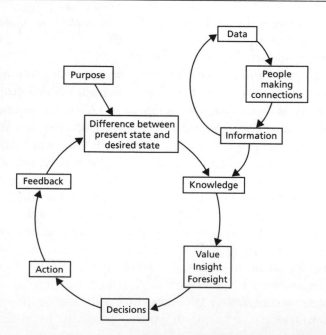

Types of Organizational Learning

Organizations can engage in simple learning, generative learning and, of course, no learning.

No Learning

Organizations, like people, can keep on doing the same ineffective actions – flogging a dead horse. When you discover you are riding a dead horse, the best strategy is to dismount. All too often organizations appoint a committee to study the horse, try to improve their riding ability or deny it is dead and say it is only resting.

Simple Learning

Simple learning serves stability and usually means setting up a procedure so that the same process can be duplicated faster, cheaper and more efficiently. This will be good in the short term. In the long term you may end up with a good, fast, cheap procedure for an out-of-date process.

Simple learning asks the question:

How can we make a procedure that will solve this problem?

Generative Learning

Here organizations question their assumptions about the market. An example was Microsoft's embracing the Internet. Before 1995, Microsoft was operating on the assumption that the Internet would not be important in computing and therefore it expended its energies on doing what it had always done very well – making operating systems for PCs. The company could have continued to build operating systems, but as the Internet became more important Microsoft completely re-evaluated its work and operating systems.

Generative learning in organizations only comes from the generative learning of the people within them.

The question for generative learning:

What are we assuming about this situation and is it
    accurate?

To manage needs only single loop learning. To lead, you need generative learning.

References

1 Dr Jens Dahlgaard, A. Norgaard and S. Jakobsen, 'Profile of success', *Journal of European Quality*, Vol.5, no.1
2 C. Argyris, R. Putnam and D. Smith, *Action Science*, Jossey-Bass, 1985. See other work by Argyris for more about single and double loop learning.

Bibliography

O'Connor, J. and McDermott, I., *The Art of Systems Thinking*, Thorsons, 1997

6

GAMES AND GUARDIANS

Rules, Laws and Boundaries

Rules are fine, but they will only stretch so far. They have to be based on shared values and consensus. Any rule without widespread support cannot be enforced without a police state. When rules are backed up by rewards and punishments, these also need the broad support of the community.

Laws apply to everybody and local rules of conduct set boundaries, they make choices easier and give some basic guidance in unfamiliar situations. You need to know the laws and customs of a foreign country, and the same principle applies when you enter any community or business. These have rules of conduct, dress codes, 'the way we do things around here' – and you ignore them at your peril. Some of these rules may be open, pinned up on the wall or part of the job description, but there will also be many informal rules that you will only learn when you have worked there for some time. Also, we set our own internal rules of conduct. These may clash with the laws and regulations – for example traffic speed limits are widely flouted and computer software is easily copied and often shared rather than bought. So, inside legal and moral rules, we set many of our own boundaries.

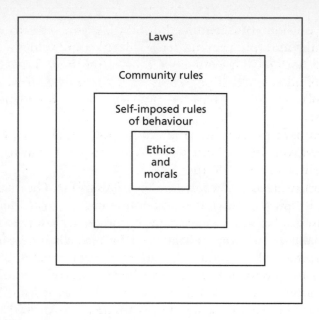

All leaders work with or outside boundaries. In the most extreme cases, leaders like Martin Luther King, Mahatma Gandhi or the Chinese student leaders in Tiananmen Square work outside the largest boundary – the laws of the country – in order to change them. They also have to work outside the other boundaries – the local community laws and their own internal rules – to do this. Some leaders work outside the local rules of their community while still inside the national laws. But all leaders have to challenge their own rules of conduct. A leader has to venture outside accepted rules and norms, not necessarily in an iconoclastic or violent way (although some leaders do), but in a spirit of exploration. Leaders journey into unknown territory – unknown for them and for the others who follow them. This means as a leader you must be ready to expand your personal boundaries, to take a risk, to do what you are afraid to do. If you want a comfortable and quiet life with no change, do not seek to be a leader (and don't follow one either).

Trust

Once outside your familiar boundaries, you have to make new rules and find what underlies all rules and values – trust. That is both trust in yourself and trust in others. Trust is the basis of all relationships. When (and if) you can trust yourself and others, you have an immense space for ideas and action.

What is trust? Another nominalization, an abstract noun. How do you think about trust? What does it mean to trust yourself or to trust another person?

Trust underlies so many leadership skills that we cannot avoid it. Also, I think it is the most important leadership quality. It takes trust in yourself to strike out on a new path, especially when others tell you to stay at home. It takes trust to follow a leader as well. 'Trust' and 'true' come from the same root. You trust what is true for you. The word comes originally from an Old Norse word *traustr*, meaning 'strong'. We trust in a person's strength, that it will not let us down, literally or metaphorically. Trust is how we deal with uncertainty.

Trust comes in two varieties. The first is trusting something that has been tried and tested. Here you are on familiar ground, which you know has had the strength to support you in the past and you trust it still has that strength. For example, you have asked a colleague to support you in a meeting and you trust he will again, because he has done so before. Or you have successfully coached many colleagues, so you trust your coaching skills. A friend tells you what happened to him and you believe him. All this comes down to trust, trust in others, trust in yourself, based on prior experience. Trust means you do not have to think, to scheme, to make contingency plans. If your friend says he will support you, you trust he will and you do not have to make plans about what you will say or do if he does not.

Second, we build trust over time – we test the strength of the support, giving it our weight and taking the risk of being let down. This is how we build relationships, gradually showing the other person more and more of ourselves. The risk comes from lack of knowledge – how much do you have to know of a person before you can trust them? Will they let you down? Will they laugh at you? Do they feel the same way about you? We usually judge by hindsight. If the relationship turns out well, then you took a well-calculated risk. If it turns out badly, then you took a foolhardy chance. At the time it was neither, just your best guess in an uncertain situation. Even when you know someone very well, they may still let you down. They may lie or they may just make a mistake. When someone lies to you, they were not trustworthy. But a mistake is an error in retrospect – literally a mis-take, 'taking' the situation the wrong way. When you say you made a mistake, you are claiming you are still trustworthy.

We have different thresholds for trust. We build these thresholds from our experience, especially our earliest experience with adults. Too low a threshold and you trust too easily, without testing for strength first, and you may be let down often. Too high a threshold and you want too much information – life history, date of birth, collar size and brand of toothpaste – before trusting someone, so very few people qualify and that can leave you emotionally isolated. Some people seesaw between the two extremes. They start too low and people take advantage of them, so they become disillusioned and decide no one is trustworthy. But with too high a threshold, they give no one a chance to prove themselves trustworthy and therefore they cannot get feedback about the best level of trust. Then they feel isolated and may think perhaps it is best to trust people after all, so they lower their guard too far and someone comes along and takes advantage again.

You do not have to trust completely or not at all, there are degrees. The best threshold is somewhere in the middle, a threshold that allows you intimacy, but keeps you safe from being exploited. There is no absolute certainty, but trust is as near as you will get with another person. Gather as much information as possible, especially if you have a lot to lose, however in the end you always have to make a leap of faith.

Leaders are realists, with trust as with anything else. They do not exude a fuzzy goodwill to all and sundry, paying no attention to experience or the evidence for their senses. To trust people indiscriminately would be naïve (and dangerous), and some people you can trust in one situation but not in another. In everyday life, we may trust someone with money but not with our spouse (or vice versa). We also judge people by what they do and what they value, before deciding to trust them in a particular situation. But how much information do you need? When do you decide enough is enough?

Do you apply Roman law or common law to trust? Whichever one you use will affect your relationships profoundly.

Common law starts with the presupposition that people are trustworthy, unless proved otherwise. People who apply common law will gather information and then, finding nothing to indicate a person is untrustworthy, will trust them. Roman law starts with the assumption that people are untrustworthy unless proved trustworthy. People applying Roman law gather information because they need to get evidence that someone is trustworthy before going ahead. This is not just a fine distinction, but a whole way of being. It will colour how you see the world and how you deal with people. Living with others means we have to have some level of trust or life would be impossible.

Leaders have to be trustworthy, because leadership means dealing with uncertainty. You have to deal with your own doubts and uncertainty, and you have to convince others. People will generally stay with what they know unless you can convince them of something better, and to convince them, you have to get them to trust you. At first a leader has to support others in their uncertainty. They need to feel your strength in order to decide that you are trustworthy. Later everyone supports each other.

There is no technique for trust, it goes beyond NLP technique. NLP uses the term 'rapport' for a relationship of trust and influence, but although this is a good first step, rapport is limited to place and time. I think that when you are trustworthy, you will have rapport, but you cannot necessarily create trust by building rapport, because rapport happens in the moment and is created for a purpose. Trust goes beyond rapport. It goes deeper because it spans all the neurological levels and it goes through time as well. Rapport is built in the short term and trust is long term. When you trust someone, you keep trusting them whether they are present or not.

NLP has many means of creating rapport by pacing all the neurological levels *(see pp.48–52)* – matching clothes, appearance and cultural mores on the environment level, matching body language, posture, gesture and voice tone on the behaviour level, matching ways of thinking, showing competence on the capability level, and particularly by matching beliefs and values. These create rapport in the moment and leaders do use these skills.

Rapport comes from an honest attempt to understand how the world is for the other person, and being willing to try and experience the world through their eyes and ears. As the Native American saying has it, 'Do not judge another person until you have walked a mile in their moccasins.' It is important to understand the people you want to influence, to show you acknowledge their beliefs and values, but understanding does not mean agreement, you do not have to agree with them. So, a person who is good at building rapport will build good relationships. However, unless they trust themselves and keep their word, they will not necessarily be trusted. Trust evokes trust.

Trust begins by trusting yourself. It comes from being clear about your own boundaries and your own values, what you will do and what you will not do. When you say you will do something, if you are trustworthy, you will keep your word. Becoming trustworthy does not mean getting people to trust you, it means becoming *worthy* of their trust, becoming the kind of person people will trust. In NLP terms, trust is an identity level value and not a capability.

Like leadership, trust turns out to be another of these nominalizations that has to be reciprocal. It does not exist in isolation. A man who trusts no one is likely to be a man whom no one trusts. But if you trust yourself then others will trust you.

The following exercises will help you clarify some of your attitudes towards trust.

Trust and Values

How do you decide whom to trust?

How do you decide when to trust?

What rules do you have about whom you trust and whom you do not?

What are your value equivalents of trust – what does someone have to do in order to be trustworthy and what do they have to do to become untrustworthy?

Do you treat people as basically trustworthy unless you have evidence otherwise or do you treat people as basically untrustworthy unless you have evidence to the contrary?

What evidence do you need?

Do you need to see it with your own eyes?

Do you believe people are trustworthy if others say so and if so, whose word do you trust?

Do you pay attention to particular neurological levels?

Are there certain environments you trust and others you do not trust?

Do you trust people from some environments and not others?

Do you trust a person in one context but not another?

Do you decide people are trustworthy by what they do, regardless of where they are or whom they are with?

Do you pay the most attention to a person's beliefs and values before deciding whether they are trustworthy or do you pay the most attention to the kind of person they are?

Exploring Trust

Think about the word 'trust'. How do you represent it
in your mind?
What feeling do you have for trust?
What qualities does it have and whereabouts in your
  body do you feel it?
What sounds or voices come to your mind when you
  think of trust?
What qualities do they have and where do they come
  from?
What picture do you have of trust?
What kind of picture is it?
What qualities does it have?
Are you in the picture or are you looking at the
  picture?
Is it a moving picture or a still picture?
Is it colour or black and white?
How big is the picture?
How far away?
Whereabouts in your visual field is it placed – to the
  right, left, up or down or straight ahead?
Think of a symbol for trust. Make it reflect the meaning
of the word 'strength'.
    Now think of yourself trusting someone.
Ask yourself the same questions:
What kind of picture do you have?
What sounds go with it?
What feelings go with it?

Building Self-Trust

Explore your own ideas of self-trust in this exercise.
Think of a model, someone you trust.
What kind of picture do you have of them?
What qualities does this picture have?
Is it a moving picture or a still picture?

Is it in colour or black and white?

How big is the picture?

How far away is it?

Whereabouts in your visual field is it placed – to the right, left, up or down or straight ahead?

What sounds are associated with the person?

Does their voice have a particular quality?

Now do the same for a person you do not trust.

What kind of picture, sounds and feelings do you have when you think of this person?

How do these pictures and sounds differ from the picture and sounds of someone you do trust?

Imagine putting the two pictures side by side next to each other. If someone who did not know either person were to look at the pictures and listen to the sounds, how would they know which person was the one you trusted?

Now imagine looking at yourself.

What qualities does your picture have?

Do you trust that person (the 'you' out there)?

Make the qualities of the picture the same as for the picture of the person you trust. You can also have your model there to support you and you can give yourself the symbol of trust that you have chosen.

Now, what qualities do you need to develop for that picture to be convincing?

Step into the picture and become yourself – trustworthy.

What does that feel like?

Does it feel different?

What do you have to do to make this self a reality?

The Prisoner's Dilemma

Misplaced trust can be very costly, but you need a minimum level of trust to do business. How far can you trust competitors? Where does the fuzzy line between legitimate competition and unfair trading begin? Even fair competition involves trust.

Trust also means co-operation, with various parties working together. But why co-operate at all? What's the point? Does it lead to any mutual advantage?

Some extremely interesting research has been done on the problems of trust and co-operation, based on a game called 'the prisoner's dilemma'.[1] Here is the game. Imagine being a freedom fighter in a corrupt regime. You are working with a new partner whom you have only just met. One day, you are both snatched by the secret police in an ambush and interrogated in separate cells. You have no way of communicating with your partner. The police interrogator offers you a diabolical deal. Inform on your partner and you will be granted immunity from prosecution, go free and get a reward. Your partner will be fined and imprisoned. They also tell you that if both you and your partner rat on each other, then neither of you gets the reward, but you will both go to jail. You also know the police have no evidence without a confession and even they cannot risk charging you if you sit tight and say nothing. If both you and your partner stay silent you will both go free to fight another day. Here's the twist. The police tell you that they have offered an identical deal to your partner.

What do you do?

The best deal from your point of view is for both of you to stay silent. But can you trust your partner? Perhaps they need the money. If you stay silent and your partner informs on you, then you will lose and they will go free and get a reward. You will be fined and imprisoned. Perhaps betraying your partner is better. But if your partner thinks you will do that, then they will inform on you first, as they have nothing to lose. Your choice depends on their choice, depends on your choice ... What's the best strategy?

Whatever you choose, you have to live with the consequences, but this is a hypothetical situation, to demonstrate the intricacies of trust and co-operation versus mistrust and non-cooperation. In a one-off play, when you have no extra information, the only rational choice is to defect and inform on your partner. But trust or mistrust comes down to a relationship, so it is more realistic to play the prisoner's dilemma game many times to find the best strategy over time.

We keep having to make the same kind of decision – can I trust you? – but with different people each time. Everyone has a 'trust trail', either a reputation for keeping their word or a trail of broken promises. If you can, you look at someone's previous track record before deciding whether to trust them. If you do not know their track record, then you have to make a best guess that depends on the circumstances and how much you have to lose.

The prisoner's dilemma game was played as part of research into game theory in the 1970s. Game theory is far from playful, it studies how we make alliances and come to decisions about our best moves when we do not have all the available information. Depending on the rules of the game, some moves gain an advantage, while others lose. To do well in any game, whether it is a friendly game of Monopoly (if it is possible to have a friendly game of Monopoly) or running an international business, you need to know the rules. Everyone has to obey the rules or there can be no game. Even international summit meetings have rules. Game theory deals with situations where there are rules and the insights were used to try to resolve the real-life political deadlocks of the time: the Cold War and the Arab–Israeli stalemate.

In the late 1970s a political researcher named Robert Axelrod wanted to find out the best strategy for winning at prisoner's dilemma, so he devised a computer tournament in Michigan. Anyone could enter a computer program that would take the place of one of the prisoners. The programs would participate in an all-play-all tournament, known as 'iterated prisoner's dilemma'. Each game with an opposing computer would consist of 200 moves, giving the computer adversaries a chance to size up the strategy of the opposing program and counter it if possible. Each program would collect a history and a reputation, just as people do. Each program was fed information on how its adversary had played previous games, so it could change its strategy based on the opponent's style (if it was programmed to do so).

The tournament was marked, the programs scored points for each round, and the scoring reflected what happens in life: when both players trust, both do equally well and there is a win-win situation. But if you trust and they double-cross you, then you lose and they win. The highest score was for defection, provided the other program did not also defect (the equivalent of informing and going free with a reward). The next highest score was for co-operation, the equivalent of both players being released from jail for not informing. Fewer points were awarded if both players defected, as both would go to jail, but at least neither was fined. Finally the lowest score was for co-operating when the other player informed. Then you were jailed and had to pay a fine as well.

	You defect	**You co-operate**
Other player defects	Both score the same (low)	Opponent scores well You score badly
Other player co-operates	You score well They score badly	Both score the same (high)

Fourteen programs were submitted, ranging from simple strategies like 'always defect' or 'always co-operate' to extremely complex ones. One strategy came out a clear winner at the end of the tournament. Can you guess what it was?

The 'nice guy' programs did not win. Indiscriminate co-operation and trust did not score highly, and I wouldn't recommend them in real life either. But neither did the non-cooperative programs. The winning program was submitted by the psychologist Anatol Rapoport from the University of Toronto. It was called 'Tit for Tat', and always began by co-operating on the first move (so it was a common law program). After that, it would do exactly the same move as its opponent had done the move before. Simple on the surface, but very effective. It started with the olive branch, always beginning with trust. After that it rewarded trust with trust, but punished non-cooperation immediately. As it was transparent and predictable, other players knew where they stood straightaway. In that important sense, it was 'trustworthy'. Since the object of the tournament was to make the highest score and a high score in any round was given for both players co-operating, it made perfect sense for the other programs to co-operate each time, giving a win-win situation. When both players trust, both score highly.

Eight of the 14 programs were 'good', meaning they never defected on the first round. All eight easily did better than the 'nasty' programs, those that did defect on the first round. In case the result was a lucky chance, the tournament was repeated. Sixty-two programs entered. 'Tit for Tat' won again. In any one game, it could lose (for example, against a program that always defected), but as a long-term strategy, it came out with the top score.

Real life is much more complex, but this elegant experiment showed that trust pays at the bottom line, regardless of how the other players act.

It is worth noting that Tit for Tat's success did not depend on the other player's strategy. Whatever the other player did, it simply mirrored it. It did not try to second-guess their strategy.

The winning strategy is clear: mutual trust pays for both players. How do you get mutual trust? By being prepared to trust first of all and being predictable in your responses. Trust evokes trust.

What would be the worst losing strategy? If you want to lose badly, start with non-cooperation, then take offence at the other player's lack of trust and use it to justify your own lack of trust and keep retaliating. Mistrust evokes retaliation, so a player who sees the world full of competitors and selfish opportunists will excite that very behaviour from others and so confirm their belief. These players never learn, because they do not connect their actions with the consequences. Clearly these players will always do worst in the long run and, like a jungle, the market is an unforgiving environment for the poorly adapted, so they will become extinct.

The leadership strategy is clear: trust and co-operate first unless you have information to the contrary. Retaliate immediately when you meet non-cooperation *and make it clear why you are doing so.* Link it clearly to the other's lack of trust. Meet trust and co-operation with trust and co-operation.

Co-operation is a pragmatic strategy; trust is enlightened self-interest.

Games and Meta Games

People mistrust others because they see the world as a 'zero sum game'. Zero sum games must have a winner and a loser. The winner wins at the loser's expense. Chess, political elections, horse races, tennis are all zero sum games – for every winner, there must be a loser. A plus and a minus makes nothing, hence the title – zero sum – nothing left over.

Zero sum games always involve these assumptions:

- Resources are scarce, there is not enough to go around and there never will be.
- Keep your strategy a secret, knowledge is power, otherwise the other players will beat you.
- Anything that hurts another player is good for you. You can win by hurting all the other players while giving away nothing yourself.

Non-zero sum games do not need to have a winner and a loser; all players may do well or badly. In these games one player's misfortune does not necessarily help others, it may actually make it harder for the other players. Markets, natural ecologies, human communication are all examples of these games, they are all built on co-operation and competition, or 'co-opetition'.

Non-zero sum games assume:

- Resources are potentially greater than any one player would need or could use.
- Everyone either has the resources they need or can create them.
- You can be doing better than your competitors and you could still all be doing really badly.
- Open strategy can be a good move – when others know what you are doing, then they can more easily plan their strategy so you both gain.

These two strategies are more than just games, they are philosophies of life. A zero sum life is stressful, busy and full of pressure and anxiety. If you are not winning then you must be losing. Such people have to win every argument. If you have ever met people like this, you know how annoying they can be. Few people will 'play' with them once they find out the sort of game they are playing.

Some games, however, really are zero sum, so take a look at the game from the outside to know what kind it is before you start. You need to be able to jump outside and look at your assumptions about what you are doing. If you cannot do this, then you are doomed to be in a *game without end*. Games without end have no rules for changing the rules, because there is no outside perspective on the game. These games share one rule – participants think they are deadly serious and not games at all.

I have met a few people who play like this. One man I remember was a foreign exchange trader working at a bank in the City of London. John enjoyed his work, even though it was stressful and meant long hours and he could quite possibly lose a few hundred thousand pounds by not paying attention. He played the markets as a zero sum game – if he did not make a profit, then he looked on it as a lost bonus. He took the same mind-set home to his family. He had to win arguments and if he did not get his own way then he would sulk. Arguments were there to win or lose, not to discover more. His children had to excel at school and sports, and if they did not, he would lecture them on how important it was to win, to come first. 'There is only one place worth having,' he would say, 'and that's first. If you're not first, you're nowhere.'

When we looked at his way of representing his work, he either had a mental picture of himself first, close, bright, high up and smiling (and felt good about it), or nowhere, lost in the dark. That picture made him feel really bad, so he worked hard to keep it at bay.

If you imagine life like this then it makes sense to try desperately to win at all costs, so we worked together initially on creating a space between these two representations, so there were some other ways to be besides 'up front and happy' or 'lost in the dark'. John also began to question his belief that life was a zero sum game, like international money markets.

Our beliefs set the rules of the games we play and we can change the game by changing our beliefs. Generative learning takes us out of the trap of playing the same game, endlessly circling the Monopoly board, bankrupt.

Games without end have rules, the most important being that you have to play under existing rules. Whenever you hear these phrases become suspicious:

'Only certain people can participate.'
'There have to be winners and losers.'
'Time is running out – we must have a result.'
'The rules cannot be changed.'

The opposite of a game without end is a *meta game*. *Meta* is a Greek word meaning 'above' or 'beyond'. Meta games have rules for changing the rules and you can make every game into a meta game if you question your assumptions. Whenever you meet a situation where what you are doing is inadequate, change the existing rules or formulate new ones. Leaders do this. It may mean questioning rules at work or it may mean questioning your own assumptions, even what kind of person you are.

Beliefs and Assumptions

We generalize from our experience to form our beliefs, and use past experience to guide us in the present and future. We have beliefs about ourselves, other people and the kind of world we live in. Our beliefs create our expectations, they are our guiding principles, they draw our boundaries, our personal borders. We take many beliefs on trust. We trust the evidence of our senses, although sometimes they can mislead us, and we trust what others tell us, even though they may be mistaken. From the inside, beliefs seem to be true. Looked at from the outside they are the ideas we trust and we act *as if* they were true. Beliefs are the individual rules we live by. What we believe decides whether we allow ourselves to live under Roman law or common law, whether we play zero sum games, meta games or games without end, and whether we can break out of the ring of simple learning into the charmed circle of generative learning. When you believe that one man's loss is another man's gain, then playing life as a zero sum game makes perfect sense. Our actions are always perfectly rational given the belief they are based on.

Our beliefs may, however, be out of date or mistaken. Considering the extent to which they influence our lives, we pay them very little attention. We never think about whether they are useful, liberating or repressive. We confuse them with facts. We consider them as unalterable as gravity, death and taxes. We are more likely to question our legislation than our beliefs, yet our beliefs are our *internal* legislation.

Imagine for a moment that you are a country. What kind of laws do you live under? Are these rules and laws just? How much freedom do they give you? Are you living under Roman law or common law, and would you be subject to

United Nations sanctions as a repressive regime, or would you be a free democracy?

In the first chapter I quoted Max de Pree: 'A leader's task is to define reality.' Now we can see it means defining our beliefs about what is possible for ourselves and making others believe that it is possible for them as well. Your beliefs about yourself and others are some of your greatest resources on the leader's journey.

Now imagine that your beliefs can be changed like the laws in a country. Look at beliefs from the outside for a moment, as the principles we act on – we act *as if* they were true. NLP talks of 'presuppositions' rather than beliefs – presuppositions are what you presuppose to be true in a situation, so you act as if they were true. At one level, we 'believe' in gravity, so we presuppose (and with good reason) that falling from the top of a building would result in serious injury. We act as if this were true and we trust gravity will not let us down, to mix a metaphor. So we take care. Our assumptions shape our actions, they make the rules and the boundaries within which we approach our problems.

Human nature is much more complex than gravity. We can evoke friendship in others by being friendly, evoke hostility by being hostile, but you don't evoke gravity. Gravity (as far as I know) is not a self-fulfilling prophecy that depends on your belief in it. I think we often approach others as if human nature and gravity were alike.

Testing Plans for Assumptions

A plan is only as good as the beliefs and assumptions it is based on. Here is one way you can check on your assumptions in any plan or decision you make. Take some time to concentrate on this process. You will need to write down your assumptions.

What are you assuming about the present situation?

What has to be true for your plan to work well?

(Another way to find assumptions is to think of

all the things that could go wrong and then the
reasons you hope those things will not happen –
these will be your assumptions.)
When you have written down your assumptions, group
them from two points of view.

First, how important is each to the success of your
plan?
Some may be essential. In other words, if you are
wrong, your plan will fail.
Others will be dispensable – you can work around them
if they turn out to be mistaken.
Give each idea a score from one to ten. Ten means they
are essential. One means they are not really necessary, you could get around them if you had to.

Secondly, how certain are you about them?
You will be 100 per cent sure of some, others you will be
less confident about. Again, give each a score from
one to ten. Ten for those you are completely sure of
and one for those you are not at all sure about.
When you have gone through each assumption from
both points of view, divide them into four groups:
Those you are confident about and are necessary to the
success of your plan go in the first group.
Those you are confident about but are unimportant go
in the second.
The third contains those you are uncertain about and
that are not important anyway.
Lastly there are those you are uncertain about that are
important. These are the ones to look at closely.
Lay them out on a graph as shown.

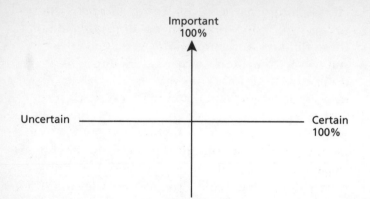

Your clusters should be in the top right and bottom left corner.

Beware if some assumptions fall in the bottom right corner (very necessary but also very uncertain). In such a case, rethink your plan, it is far too risky.

Also beware if most of your assumptions seem to fall into one category.

If they're all in the certain and unnecessary group, then look further – you have probably forgotten something significant, or some are not as certain as you think they are.

What presuppositions would be helpful for leaders? What guiding principles best govern a leader? You do not have to believe them, but if you act *as if* they were true you will find out what works best. What we trust in becomes true for us.

Leaders' Presuppositions: Your Internal Statute Book

These would be some of my suggested presuppositions for leaders. If you act as if these were true, you will be acting as a leader. See how these fit with your own internal statute book. What others can you add?

- I can and I will achieve my goals. They are not impossible.
- I have all the resources I need, or can acquire them.
- Others also have all the resources they need, or can acquire them.
- I am trustworthy.
- Others are trustworthy unless I have evidence to the contrary.
- Understanding comes from action, not logical thought.
- Everyone is doing the best they can given the situation they are in.

When you change your guiding principles, you engage in generative learning and you get new insights.

> Think of a difficult situation with another person for a moment. Imagine a typical scene that demonstrates the problem.
> Once again, how do you think about it? What picture are you making?
> Is it in colour or black and white?
> Is it moving or still?
> How far away is it?
> Whereabouts in space is it in relation to you – in front, up, down, to one side or the other?
> Are you observing the picture or are you in it, looking at it through your own eyes?
> Are there sounds in this scene?
> What is the quality of the sounds? How loud are they?
> Are there any voices?
> How do you feel about the scene?

> Blank out the memory and come back to the present moment. Look around you and remember where you are here and now.
> What do you want to achieve in this situation?

> Now take one of the leadership principles that naturally appeals to you – maybe the idea that you have all the re-

sources you need, or can acquire them, or that the other person has all the resources they need. It could be that everyone is doing the best they can in the situation they are in. Imagine the situation as a civil dispute. What rule are you going to apply to it?

See the situation through the filter of that idea. How is it different? How would that situation change if you acted as if this principle were true? Would the other person be able to maintain what they are doing in the same way? Would you?

Imagine yourself in that problem situation with that principle. What new possibilities are there?

Pick at least two other ideas and go through the same process. You can use some of the leaders' presuppositions or any other powerful idea that attracts you. What new ways of action open out?

Now imagine the next time you confront that person. What will you be doing differently? Think of yourself in that situation, speaking in a new way. What reaction do you think you will get?

How has the problem changed now when you think about it?

How do you feel about it now?

A new way of thinking is the most powerful resource you have. It automatically opens up space for both yourself and others, because your assumptions about others shape how you approach the situation and so they will also shape the response you get. Broadening your thinking gives everyone more space.

You can use these ideas to help other people in ordinary conversation. Ask them what they assume about the situation or what they think is true about the other person. Ask them how the situation would be different if they thought about it in another way and either suggest one of the leaders' presuppositions or ask them to think of a time when they dealt very successfully with a difficult situation. What did they assume about the other people in that situation that allowed them to resolve it? Then ask them to think about the present situation in the same way.

Most problems with others come about because we do not see the situation in the same way that they do and we think we are right. We look at our own actions and they make perfect sense (and they *do* – if the assumptions that they are based on are trustworthy).

We judge ourselves by our intentions. From our point of view, our intentions are good. We are trying to get something we value. And we think we are reasonable – given the circumstances, there did not seem to be a better choice, otherwise we would have taken it. If we hurt someone or what we do turns out badly, then it was a mistake, or at worst, we accuse ourselves of being thoughtless. Mistakes can only be judged in retrospect – actions did not turn out as planned, there was a side-effect, someone reacted badly or we did not have all the information. An apology is a plea for our honesty, it does not change the mistake. We apologize for the result, not for the action we took.

From our viewpoint, then, what we do makes perfect sense, *but we do not give others the same benefit of the doubt.* Usually not understanding their goals or values, or how they see the world, we seldom judge them by their intentions, but by their results. We also tend to take things personally. Another person's mistake is not just a mistake, it's personal, it affects us. What they do may also challenge our beliefs, expectations and trust. When we feel hurt, we often assume the other person deliberately meant to hurt us, or if not, they were at best stupid and incompetent. But they may not have meant to affect us at all, just get something of value to themselves. Everybody is a hero in their own story, even when they have a starring role as a villain in another person's story. Just as we are judging our own actions by our intentions and the actions of others by the results, so others are busy doing the same, judging themselves on their intentions and judging us on the results. It's not surprising that misunderstandings and blame abound.

What does this mean with regard to leadership? The meaning of any communication is both the intention *and* the result, depending on how you look at it. Leaders influence others, so while they are clear about their intentions, they are more interested in the effect of what they do as seen from the other person's point of view. They judge communication by the results.

Also, leaders don't confuse informing with communicating. Informing means telling. Communicating means sharing the message. The message has to be received, otherwise it is not properly communicated, and that means putting it in a way the other person can understand. When you want to be understood in a foreign country, you have to phrase it in their language (or at least try to). Sign language and Esperanto only go so far. Leaders don't use the excuse 'I told them to do it, but they didn't!' This is the equivalent of the doctor's classic 'The operation was a success but the patient died!'

Leaders don't blame. They take results as feedback, learn from them and help others to learn. For example, what happens when you see someone make a mistake?

Do you punish them?
Do you try to ignore it?
Do you help them so they don't do it again?
Does it vary depending on who makes the mistake?
    Your child?
    Your partner?
    A work colleague?
    Your boss?
And if you have different responses, why?
What would happen if you swapped these responses around?
    For example, if you responded to a work colleague's
    mistake as you would to your partner's mistake?

An acquaintance of mine is very tolerant at work. He's a fashion designer and many staff depend on him for ideas and guidance. I know he gives them a very free hand, lets them run with their own ideas and supports them if they fail. He says this develops his employees so they work well and enjoy what they do. He also has a teenage son. He helps his son and gives him a lot of advice, mostly 'Don't do this' and 'Make sure you don't do that.' And his son complains that he is always being criticized. Father denies being critical, he says he just wants to help, but nothing his son does quite makes the grade. He was complaining to me recently that his son was resentful and wouldn't accept help and he hated to see him do badly. I asked him casually what he would do if his son were an employee. He fell silent, thought for a moment and then changed the subject. Over the next few months he became more relaxed and permissive with his son and their relationship improved.

The Channel of Experience

How can our intentions be so badly misunderstood? How can intention and result miss each other so badly? You have no doubt marvelled at how some people can so completely misunderstand what you say and do, and I assure you that you have amazed them in the same way. Understanding (and misunderstanding) happens in an instant. How?

First, we have limited attention, so we select from all possible experience. A video camera and a tape recorder would capture much more. Then we make meaning of that selection. Some of these are individual meanings based on our experience, others cultural meanings, based on general expectations. For example, when someone yawns, we generally interpret this to mean they are either bored or tired. Then we use these meanings to draw conclusions about others and ourselves. In this case you could conclude that you were boring this person, or that they were tired (which has nothing to do with you), or that they were rude, or even that they were interested in what you were saying and wanted to get more oxygen to their brain to understand it better. It is hard to take any event just as an event. We are the centre of our universe and so it seems everything must have a personal meaning.

As a result of these meanings, we may react emotionally. If we thought someone was bored by what we were saying, we might feel angry, or threatened, or disheartened, or inadequate. When we have repeated experiences of this nature, or maybe one very strong impression, we generalize and build a belief about the kind of person we are. And, as we have seen, our beliefs lead to our actions.[2]

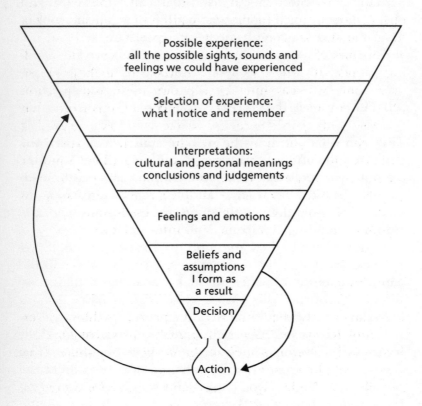

The channel of experience

The diagram shows that only the first step (possible experience) and the last step (action) are visible to others. The rest takes place inside our heads, according to our own rules.

Secondly, it gets narrower and narrower – there are many possible experiences but only one action comes out at the end, as if all our experiences have been squeezed down an ever-narrowing funnel until a tiny trickle emerges from the end. Thirdly, the actions are feedback that may reinforce those selections and so bolster those beliefs (first order learning), or cause me to re-evaluate my beliefs (second order learning), and that leads to different actions and eventually to a different selection of my experience.

This model suggests three ways to avoid misunderstandings, especially when someone hurts your feelings. First, trace your own reasoning in your own mind and question whether you have drawn reasonable conclusions from what you saw and heard. Secondly, make your own reasoning clear. Say what you noticed and the conclusions you drew and how you feel about that (if appropriate). Check whether the meaning you make is actually what the other person intended. Thirdly, check other people's reasoning. Ask them to describe how they came to their conclusions and see whether there is any merit in their interpretation.

References

1 For an exhaustive treatment of the prisoner's dilemma see Anatol Rapoport, Albert Chammah and Carol Orwant, *Prisoner's Dilemma: A Study in Conflict and Co-operation*, University of Michigan Press, 1965.

  See also Dudley Lynch and Paul Kordis, *The Strategy of the Dolphin*, Ballantine Books, 1988.

2 I am indebted to Chris Argyris for his work on the 'ladder of inference'. See his *Overcoming Organizational Defences*, Prentice Hall, 1990.

  Also, see page 242 *et seq.* in *The Fifth Discipline Fieldbook* by Peter Senge, Charlotte Roberts, Richard Ross, Bryan Smith and Art Kleiner, Doubleday, 1994.

Bibliography

Fukuyama, Francis, *Trust: The Social Virtues and the Creation of Prosperity*, 1996

Bateson, G., *Steps to an Ecology of Mind*, Jason Aronsen, 1987

Carse, James, *Finite and Infinite Games*, Penguin, 1986

Rapoport, Anatol, 'Escape from paradox', *Scientific American* 217, July 1967, 50–6

Watzlawick, Paul, *Munchausen's Pigtail*, W. W. Norton, 1990

7

CHANGE AND CHALLENGE

Every leader faces the same challenge: how to make a change that makes a difference. Leaders want to change the world (or part of it), overcoming outer obstacles to their vision, and that means changing themselves, overcoming inner weaknesses, embodying new skills, learning new values and creating and being comfortable with their own style of leadership.

The challenge for business leaders is to be a combination of warrior and prophet, delivering high performance in the business and trying to get a competitive edge by trying to anticipate the market. Business has to continually change in small ways to stay competitive and may have to change drastically in response to outside conditions. The question is not whether to change, but how much change to allow for.

Business leaders need to manage two types of change. 'First order change' is change *in* the system, for example, changing procedures, management styles, recruiting policies, sales methods and marketing targets while the core business remains the same. This is also called 'transitional change'. Sometimes sufficient first order change triggers 'second order change'. Second order change is change *of* the system and is often called 'transformational change'. Examples are mergers, takeovers, new markets, new products or having to reorganize in the face of market shifts. A leader must make sure that there is enough first order change to keep the company viable and drive any second order change that is required.

Change can also take place widely across the organization, affecting everyone, or deeply, affecting only small parts but changing them radically. In the diagram, most first order change is in sector 1 – narrow and shallow. Most second order change will fall in sector 4 – wide and deep.

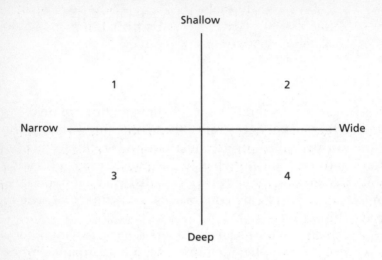

Organizational change

Change can be slow or sudden. I heard of a large food manufacturing company that needed to change considerably to meet new market conditions. It had a long history and was proud of its traditions. A new Australian CEO was appointed to shake up the company, and he chose an unconventional and very effective approach. He moved the entire company headquarters to a new building far away from the old one. Everyone wondered what he would do with the old corporate headquarters, which had been built by the founder of the firm many years ago. He actually dynamited it, videotaped the explosion and sent everyone in the organization a copy of the tape.

This man certainly made his point, but change does not have to be so explosive. Mostly it has to be gradual but guided. Businesses are easy to change if you have the authority, but it may not be so easy to keep the changes in place. Even our Australian CEO will have to be careful that his business, recently ensconced in its gleaming high-technology new headquarters, does not revert to trading in its familiar traditional hallowed way. To make a change with the least effort, and to make the change stick, you need to understand how the system works, which brings us to the third leadership skill: systemic thinking.

Systems Thinking

What is systems thinking? It is predicting and influencing a system by understanding its underlying structure. What is a system? It is an entity that works as a whole through the interaction of its parts. Our bodies are systems, made up of smaller systems – the circulatory system, the digestive system and the nervous system. Our beliefs and values are a system. Our business organizations are complex systems. We live in systems – the natural environment, the weather, even the solar system – and take part in political, economic and religious systems. We deal with systems all the time, it is only when we try to change them that we feel their power. Systems are not as simple as they often look and they refuse to behave in neat, straightforward, linear ways. Trying to change them may result in them slipping back to where they were originally or cause unwanted, unforeseen side-effects. So, leaders cannot effectively change anything, either themselves or their business, without working with some aspects of systems thinking.

A system always does more than the sum of its parts. Understanding the connections between the parts is the key to understanding how a system works. We are taught analytic thinking – breaking things down into parts in order to understand them – but analysis can never give understanding, it cannot tell you how the system works when it all works together. The ability to see how the parts fit together into a whole is *synthesis*. Analysis gives description. Synthesis gives understanding.

A system works when all the parts are working together and if any part does not work well, the whole system can be affected. In a business, when marketing or customer service do not work well, there are repercussions for the whole company. One wrong person in the wrong job can have far-reaching effects on morale. A system generally works as well as the weakest part allows it to. A computer gives a good analogy. A machine with a really fast processor but too little memory will not work up to the speed of the processor. The whole computer system will work as fast as its slowest part. So, when you want to improve a system, fix the weak link in the chain. Every part that is connected with that part, however tenuously, will work a little better and the effect will be magnified.

The reverse is also true – a part that works significantly better than the rest can also be a problem. A computer with a really fast processor but an inadequate cooling system will break down. The manufacturing division of a business with a highly successful marketing department may not be able to keep up with the demand it creates. An excellent sales department is being 'too excellent' if it generates orders that manufacturing cannot handle. This results in plenty of dissatisfied customers and ultimately fewer orders – the whole system (and that includes the customers) corrects the problem eventually. So individual success does not mean success for the whole system, as it may put too much strain on another part. Too good is not good enough.

Obvious solutions do not work for systems. I like the example from traffic control. In the late 1960s the city planners in the German town of Stuttgart tried to ease traffic congestion in the town centre by adding a street, but the traffic got worse. Adding roads to an already congested network slows it down further because of the increase in the number of junctions.

For any system to work smoothly the parts have to communicate, so systems thinking concentrates on the relationship and communication between the parts. However well a single part works, it must connect to, and communicate with, the rest of the system for the whole system to work well. Working well means working together. In a business, it comes down to people talking to each other and sharing information.

Because of the connections and communication in a system you can never just do one thing. The effects of decisions ripple outwards, like dropping a stone into a pool. Systems thinking means seeing patterns – how what you do comes back to you to influence your next move. It means thinking in circles rather than straight lines – circles rippling outwards, and circles of cause and effect where the effect of one decision becomes the cause of the next.

Communication itself is an example. When you talk to someone, they hear you, react to your voice tone and body language, and reply. You respond to what they say and decide what to say next by how they reacted to what you said previously. The conversation flows as a circle, because their response is feedback to you about what you have said, and what you say is feedback to them. A favourable response encourages you to continue the conversation along the same lines as before. When someone does not reply, we draw conclusions from it, just as when they do reply. We cannot *not* communicate – we make meaning of every response, including no response.

When you get a hostile response, it makes sense to do and say something different, yet there are too many examples of people doing the same thing harder, or doing twice as much, and expecting a different response. Take into account the feedback you are getting and try something different if necessary.

Perspectives

Think of looking at a complex system like looking at an unknown object that has at least five dimensions. One viewpoint gives just one perspective, true from that angle, but an incomplete picture of the whole object. You need the details *and* the big picture *and* a view in depth, so you need many perspectives.

With a system there is no 'right' perspective. You build your understanding from multiple perspectives. All are partially true and all are limited. NLP supplies three of these perspectives.

First, you have your own view of any situation – your own beliefs, opinions and values. This is how it appears to you; you are in your own reality, with its characteristic and familiar filters and ways of evaluating. Like it or not, it's yours. NLP calls this 'first position'.[1] Leaders need a strong first position. They need to know themselves and their values so they can be an effective role model and influence others by example.

Leaders don't, however, need to know themselves to the degree of imposing their reality on everyone else. They need to periodically clamber out of first position and imagine what it is like to be in someone else's shoes. NLP calls this 'second position' – the ability to make a creative leap of imagination to understand the world from another person's point of view, to think in the way they think. Second position is the basis of empathy and rapport, and with it comes the skill to pace others. It gives us the ability to appreciate other people's feelings. Understanding how other people feel is the first step towards leading them where they want to go.

'Third position' is a step outside your view and the other person's view to a detached perspective. There you can see the connection and relationship between the two viewpoints.

I would add two more perspectives to these three. There is another jump to a fourth position that lets you see your relationship in the context of a wider system. For example, suppose you quarrel with another manager. You know your own point of view – you think he is overbearing. You go to second position and understand that he sees you as too sensitive. Neither of these opinions is 'true', they are just points of view. You go to third position and see that the more overbearing he becomes, the quieter you become and the more you resent his attitude. The quieter you become, the more he tries to push you to become more outgoing. Now you can see that relationship in the context of the business, how your antipathy towards each other affects your team and your department, and maybe the whole business. This fourth position is a more objective view, uncoloured by personal feelings, and this can be valuable.

You can never come to a *completely* objective view, however, because you are always part of some system and you cannot take a view outside yourself, for there would be no self to take the view. You can be 'objective' only by defining the system you are outside.

Finally there is a fifth perspective: one that goes through time. The first four perspectives make up a snapshot of one moment in time. To gain the best understanding you want to see how they change over time, track the ramifications into the future and also perhaps understand how the situation built up in the first place by tracing the threads back into the past.

You cannot get the last two perspectives without the first three. You must know your own mind and you must know the other person's position and the relationships between them, before you can see them in context and through time.

Take as many perspectives as you need to understand a situation. When analysing a business problem, look at the perspectives of different stakeholders – customers, senior management, middle managers, strategic partners, suppliers and competitors. Exactly which perspectives you take will depend on the problem you are considering.

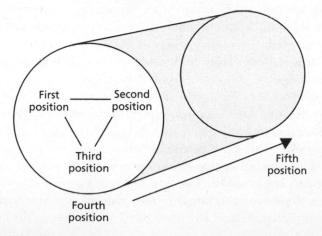

Perspectives Exercise

Use this process to understand and deal with a difficult relationship at work.

What is the problem from your point of view?
What are you trying to achieve that is important to you?
How would you describe what the other person is
    doing?

Now take second position with the other person.
Pretend you are them.

How do they see the situation?
What are they trying to achieve that is important to
    them?
How would they describe what you are doing?
Now switch to third position. Imagine seeing both your-
self and the other person from a detached, calm point
of view.

What sort of relationship exists between you?
How are you both sustaining the problem by the way
    you are acting?
If you changed what you were doing, how would the
    other person change?
What would be the benefits to you if that situation
    changed?
Are those benefits worth changing the way you are
    acting?

Now look at your relationship in the context of the
business system.
Who else is affected by that relationship?
How has the structure of the business contributed to
    that problem?
How does your relationship with that person impact
    on the business?

How far are your disagreements fuelled by the way the
   business is set up?
How far does your relationship reflect the relationship
   between the different parts of the business you are
   part of?
Has it built up gradually or did it happen suddenly?
If this situation were to continue, what might the
   longer-term impact be?
Do you need to do anything about this situation right
   now?
If nothing changes, when in the future will it be
   essential to change this situation?

A few years ago I was engaged as a consultant by an organization based in Germany. The head of department told
me the work he wanted done and then passed on the
details of the contract to the personnel department. Time
passed, nothing happened and I started to worry. I telephoned them to check that all was going smoothly and they
assured me the contract would be ready shortly. Still nothing. Weeks dragged on. From first position I was concerned
that the contract would not go through and I was annoyed
at the seemingly endless delay. The personnel department
was very apologetic whenever I spoke to them, but they
seemed incapable of speeding up the process. Taking second position with them, I sensed that they were as
frustrated with the delay as I was, but no one there had
the power to do anything about it. My telephone calls were
having no effect.

From third position it seemed that we were frozen in a pattern of frustration, delay and apology. I stopped calling
because it was a waste of time and frustration slipped into
resignation.

The contract was eventually approved and some months
later I discovered that every outside consultant's contract
had to be approved by 12 different people! The majority
were not even part of the personnel department. No wonder
it took so long.

From fourth position, this was an interesting systemic problem for the whole organization and it could not be solved by the personnel department or by me. A situation had evolved over the years whereby all the major political groups in the organization wanted to have some control over the hiring of outside consultants. The paperwork had to pass over 12 desks and some of the occupants of those desks were bound to be away or on holiday, and this created a long and tedious process. Why did they tolerate the situation? Everyone knew there was too much bureaucracy, but no department or political group was willing to sacrifice their control, symbolized by their signature on the contract, in order to bring about an easier and quicker procedure. There had clearly been some historical power struggle here that had been resolved by giving everyone a say in the contract. Their beliefs about the importance of outside consultants and what might happen if they were not informed had spawned an elaborate procedure that nobody wanted.

I think this example tells us a lot about what can go wrong in business systems. First there is what I call the 'appendix effect'. The appendix is a small protrusion we all have at birth, near the end of the large intestine in the groin area. It has no function that we know of, but it can be life-threatening if it becomes infected. Presumably at one time in our evolutionary history it had a use, but we have outgrown it. Other parts of our digestive system have taken over its function. Most business systems have the equivalent of an appendix and some have several – procedures that were instituted in the past, perhaps for a good reason, but now the organization has moved on and the procedure has not. It remains as a possible source of trouble and resentment, but the business is loath to have it out because it is deeply embedded in other procedures. This 12-signature nonsense looked to me like a typical business appendix.

Another interesting point was that no one person was to blame for the delay. The 12 individuals may well have resented the extra work involved in looking over the contract. The personnel department was as inconvenienced by the procedure as I was. In the past they had lobbied to change it – not surprisingly, as it was they who always bore the brunt of the consultants' frustration. That personnel department was as much a victim of the system as I was, and this brings us to another counter-intuitive aspect of systems: the part that breaks down or has the most difficulty is nearly always an innocent party. It is the weak point that breaks under the strain, like a pipe that gives under too much pressure. You can keep repairing the burst pipe, but unless you reduce the pressure, it will simply burst again. If you repair it really well, or replace it, the pressure will find the next weakest point and cause a blowout there. Getting angry at the pipe will do no good – the basic problem is too much pressure.

Think of this metaphor when next a department or person comes under pressure. The way the business functions may put too much pressure on people and then they are blamed for the inevitable error. People usually do the best they can in the system they are in, but they are often blamed for poor decisions, when they themselves made the best decision they could in the circumstances. If this happens often enough, they adopt a 'safety first' policy ('If it isn't working, do it twice as hard, twice as often or twice as fast') and this leads to organizational inertia.

A business culture where short-term heroic efforts are continually rewarded is a business in long-term trouble. A business culture that rewards firefighting is bound to have a way of lighting fires in the first place so someone can be heroic and put them out. Ironically, no one is rewarded for preventing problems, only for fixing them, so a leader may have a low profile because their business (or their life) runs smoothly.

What can leaders do to ensure that the business does run smoothly and that there are no fires to be fought? First, pay attention to the relationships that they are building between people. How easily can people communicate? There are two channels to pay attention to: the formal methods – the telephone, fax, e-mail, memos, meetings and reports – and the informal talks and exchange of opinions. Office space is often a metaphor that shows how people are communicating.

I remember going into one company to do some training in communication skills and was struck by how everyone had their own little cubicle, cut off from everyone else. The communal coffee room had just been demolished and replaced by a coffee machine in the name of more efficient work. But a system works as well as the parts *work together*.

Secondly, remember people do as well as the system allows them to. When you find a problem, look at the deeper level – how is it maintained in the here and now? This takes away blame. Remember that too often we do not match people to the kinds of jobs available. Some work is intrinsically demanding and needs high-calibre people. Other work might be better designed, so it can be done well by anyone, thereby releasing the creative talents of the people involved to more important matters.

Thirdly, step outside the system periodically to see how well it is working. Stepping outside and seeing the structure and the rules in operation means that in that instant you are not subject to them and have the possibility of change.

Lastly, beware the obvious solution. Look more deeply. Question the assumptions that drive your decisions. For example, conventional wisdom says that growth is good and expanding revenues will bring higher profits, but this is not so in every case.

Remember what happened to Gucci, an international name in luxury leather goods. In the mid-1980s the company launched a range of lower priced canvas goods and marketed them aggressively in large department stores and duty free shops. It also licensed its name to be used on watches and perfumes. The idea was to increase sales and thereby increase profits. The first half worked. Sales did increase, but the cost was high. Gucci lost its luxury brand image and lost sales on its main expensive lines. The net result was an increase in sales but a loss in revenue. The company attracted many new customers, but lost the more profitable established ones. Here is a salutary example of the importance of anticipating side-effects. If the company had taken second position with its customers and considered the effects of its new market strategy on them, it might have avoided this mistake.

Cause and Effect

When you stop thinking too soon, as Gucci did, you have a misleading straight line of cause and effect. This does not show how the effect can be the cause of another effect that may totally change the picture. For example, downsizing by shedding jobs is an obvious way to reduce company costs – but only if you think in straight lines. This logic ignores productivity, which is likely to suffer, as is morale and the quality of the work. Systems thinking looks for loops of multiple cause and effect, not straight lines.

To follow the possible effects of this example further still, having fewer people may lead to new procedures being installed to cope with the increased workload and this may lead to customers waiting longer, or higher prices, or lower quality still (or all three). Customers then become dissatisfied and vote with their feet, drifting away to competitors. This leads to another crisis and the company may decide that they did not downsize enough last time and repeat their mistake, heading into a downward spiral. Lowering labour costs is not necessarily a good strategic move. There are other ways to compete –through service, added value and innovation. Downsizing would only work here if everything else stayed exactly the same – in other words, the remaining people did the same quality and quantity of work that was done before.

'Everything else being equal' is a deadly phrase. Everything else is never equal. Whenever you hear that slippery phrase, think again. It is never true. Whatever you change in a system, there are always side-effects. Often, those effects interfere with your proposed solution. Sometimes they actually make the problem worse or, worst of all, the 'solution' becomes a bigger problem than the original problem.

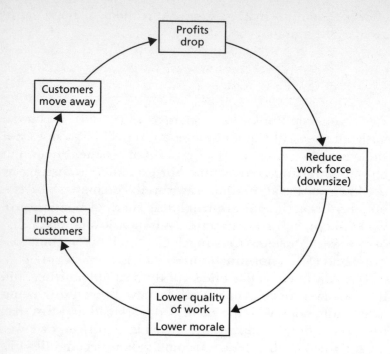

Straight-line thinking has three main flaws. First, it can be flipped around and still make sense. Does unemployment cause depression or does depression cause unemployment? They are connected, but a connection is not a cause. Second, both may equally be the effects of another unknown cause. Third, where do you stop? For example, a manager makes a wrong decision. Was it their fault? Or were they badly advised? But who appointed the advisors? Who appointed the appointee? And so on. When you go hunting causes to blame, you lose focus on the dynamic patterns that are maintaining the problem here and now. Leaders don't search for culprits, but look to change the factors that are maintaining the problem.

Unfortunately, complex systems are not easy to understand. Faced with an uncertain world, leaders have to learn to tolerate ambiguity, even to be comfortable with it. There are few easy answers.

Our formal schooling does not help us come to terms with this. From our first days at school we are asked for 'right' answers and the deeper lesson we take to heart is that every problem has a right answer, somewhere, somehow, if only we could find it. Our schooling feeds us with bounded, structured problems, then releases us into the messy world of unbounded, unstructured problems.

Leaders know a frantic hunt for 'the best' is the enemy of 'the good enough' and that there are very few problems with a right or wrong answer. Most of the time there is only a 'best available' answer – and that depends on who and where you are. Perfection is the enemy of the good. 'Good enough' works and in business a company simply has to be as good or better than the opposition.

Here is a story of two multinational CEOs who went on an African safari adventure holiday together. They both wanted a closer view of the wild animals so they sneaked into the bush, away from the safety of the tour guide. Pretty soon they were having a close encounter with a large lion. The lion looked them over and licked its lips, and they had the horrible realization that they were bottom in the immediate food chain and the safety of the Land Rover was over 100 yards away. One of the men kicked off his shoes, dropped his camera and backpack and got ready to run.

'Don't be an idiot,' hissed his companion. 'You can't outrun a lion!'

'I don't have to outrun a lion,' said the first man. 'I only have to outrun you!'

Thinking in Circles

One widely used way of analysing and dealing with a business issue is to make a list of the key factors then put them in order of importance and allocate resources or teams to improve them. This is sometimes called 'laundry list' thinking.

Laundry list thinking works well for structured, bounded problems – clear problems with one right answer. It does not work well for unstructured, unbounded problems where the problem is not clear and there is no single right answer. First, there is no guarantee that you have all the factors. There is no 'master' list to check against. Secondly, the list ignores the relationships between the factors. It is like listing a group of numbers without saying whether you add them, subtract them or multiply them.

When this type of thinking is applied, although each factor may improve, the overall result may still disappoint. Also, when resources are moved back once the project is over, the initial problem may return. A better way to think about problems is by looking at how the factors relate so that you can create a series of loops.

From Straight Lines to Loops

Think of a new initiative you want to take.

Brainstorm a list of key factors and put them in order of priority.

Then, starting with the top factor, aim to create a self-reinforcing loop by asking:

What would lead to this factor growing and being self-sustaining?

How can I link it to other factors in a way that leads to growth?

Aim to create a series of loops that will maintain or increase the key factors. Where would be the best place to allocate your resources?

Often the best place to spend your time and money is not on the top priority factor, but on another further down the list because it will cause a chain reaction that will lead to your top priority growing automatically. This lower priority factor is the leverage point. It may not be obvious.

Look for side-effects as well.

Could these factors also work against each other?

How can you arrange your resources so they work together?

I used all these ideas to look for leverage when I was working with the United Nations Industrial Development Organization (UNIDO), helping them design a workshop to explore developmental co-operation projects in developing countries. UNIDO, like other development agencies, has been using objectives oriented project planning (OOPP) to formulate and implement development projects. This method has three main steps:

- analysis of the problems of the main stakeholders (government, bankers, industrialists, technology and training institutions, etc.)
- analysis of their objectives
- planning how to achieve these objectives[2]

The project would be identified and researched and then UNIDO would run a short workshop for two to three days in the country with representatives of the key stakeholders – central government, local government, bankers, industrialists and the target benefit group. UNIDO trainers would facilitate the workshop, bring together the parties, establish how they could work together, find out the existing problems and then develop the project after establishing a working relationship with the stakeholders. UNIDO Quality Assurance was satisfied with OOPP as a broad working method, but not satisfied with what happened after the workshop. The results of the work were not sustained, the stakeholders did not feel committed, they did not feel they owned the project and many projects had little or no developmental impact.

The project I was working on was to encourage small entrepreneurs in the development of the textile and metalworking industries in Uganda.

Three areas of the workshop needed looking at. First, in previous workshops, too much time had been taken up mulling over present problems. People would blame each other, everyone would talk at length about what was wrong and little time would be spent on actually finding a way forward. So the first step was to change the workshop format so that it focused more on the future desired goal and not so much on the present problems. This was partly because the participants were invited to explore the problems first, rather than the desired outcome. We addressed this by changing the order of questions in the workshop so the first question the delegates discussed was: 'What do you want?' When this had been fully explored, the next question was about the barriers to the desired situation. Now the problems were put in context and only relevant problems were discussed. The third question was: 'How will you get what you want?' The facilitators would structure the answers into a series of steps, starting with the present and ending in the desired state. Then everyone would identify those actions the group could do on their own and those things that needed external support and finance from UNIDO.

The second problem was that the workshops often did not lead to sustainable projects. When the UNIDO facilitators left, the stakeholders did not have enough energy, commitment and momentum to carry the project through on their own.

We realized that we were looking at too narrow a part of the system. The workshop was the focal point, but only one part of the whole developmental co-operation process. We needed to put it in the context of the whole system and look at what preceded and followed it in order to make the whole process give better results. So we looked at how the workshop participants were recruited. Who was selected? How were they prepared? We discovered we knew far too little about the participants, their goals, their expectations and their understanding of the whole process. Suitable participants were not always identified; some participants were not the best people to have at the workshop while other key players were missing.

Participants were selected and interviewed by consultants in the country many weeks before the workshop. We needed to give the consultants better guidelines on selecting and interviewing prospective participants. They needed a better appreciation of the whole system: target beneficiaries, other stakeholders and external agencies such as UNIDO. They also needed guidance on how to conduct the interviews. We designed a series of questions they could use to elicit good information from the participants – their goals, values, present difficulties, the resources they needed and any possible advantages they saw in the present situation. What had been missing was a clear second position from the participants.

The third area was leadership. Sustainable change needs leadership. UNIDO facilitators needed to model leadership skills and the workshop participants needed leadership skills to drive the initiative on their own and continue the changes that the workshop had started. They needed to develop a vision. The UNIDO workshop had to spend more time helping them anticipate the future, mentally rehearsing, thinking of the possible problems and exploring solutions in advance – a process called 'future pacing' in NLP. Once the workshop was over, UNIDO had to keep the connection alive to encourage and support the initial enthusiasm that brought them to the workshop. We even looked at holding three separate workshops, one for the target beneficiaries on their own (in this case small business entrepreneurs), another with the other stakeholders and a third for all the stakeholders, specifically to identify areas where external help was needed.

When we looked at the whole system over time, helping the participants develop as leaders was the area with the most potential for change.

1. What do you want?

2. What is the present situation?

3. How can you move towards what you want?

Participation	——————— Workshop ————▶	Commitment
Selection		Sustainable change
Expectations		Leadership
Interiews		

Boundaries and Horizons

Systems change over time and it takes time for the effects to show up in the system. The further you can see into the past and into the future, the more useful connections you can make to the present. Boundaries are really horizons – look a little bit further and you will see over them.

Often we do not look far enough to see causes and patterns and so we do not learn from our experience. In systems an effect can occur a long time after its cause because it takes time to work its way around the system. We get a very real experience of this when we do hard physical work one day but our muscles do not feel it until the next day. Suppose we did not feel it for a week? How easy would it be to connect with the work we did a week ago?

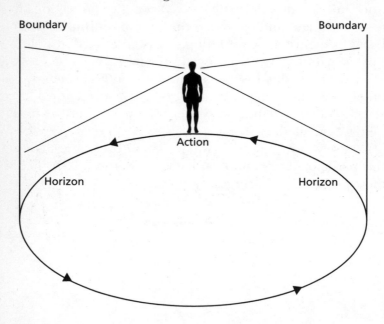

In business, because feedback from actions can take a long time to appear, managers are sometimes promoted too soon. Yet what looks like success in the short term may have left a long-term legacy of problems. Just like pushing a row of dominoes, it takes time for the impetus to work its way around, but eventually the consequences of the push come back later and surprise you. The manager we see here wants to expand his business, but has a limited perspective, he does not see beyond the boundary of the one visible domino. He pushes it and this gives him more space immediately. He has solved the problem – perhaps he is congratulated and promoted. But all the time the dominoes are falling. The new manager takes over his position and has to deal with the opposite wall falling down. He may even be blamed for the collapse.

The domino effect

Principles of Systems Thinking

- Look at the relationships between the parts as well as the parts themselves. A system works as well as the parts work together.
- Treat boundaries as horizons. What is over the other side?
- Look to the long term as well as the short term. There are delays in a system and the effect may come some time after the cause.
- Look at the details and the big picture, and how the two relate.
- Think in circles – how the effect of one action can be the cause of another. Systems work through feedback – the results of your actions coming back to you to determine your next action.
- The structure of the system determines what happens. Change the structure and you will change the result.
- When you want to make a change, think about what stops the change from happening. It is usually better to remove the barriers to change so it can happen naturally than push it through in a proactive way.
- Small changes can produce large results if you find the right place to make the change.
- Look for side-effects. When you make a change in a system everything else will not stay the same.
- The best may be the enemy of the good enough.
- Pressure appears in the weakest part, not the part that is to blame.
- Take as many perspectives as possible to understand the system.

Blame and Responsibility

Blame comes from straight-line cause-effect thinking coupled with a confusion between intention and result. Leaders take and give responsibility, not blame. Responsibility means *the ability to respond*. Blame is tempting but leads nowhere. It brings you no nearer to understanding, nor does it help solve the problem.

My experience in ordering from a computer company made me think about blame from a customer's point of view. My computer keyboard was becoming more and more unreliable and was clearly on its last legs. I ordered a new one from a telephone order company, but it was faulty, so I telephoned customer service to get a replacement as soon as possible. I was in a hurry – I had several urgent reports to research.

The customer service representative who took the call was not allowed to authorize a replacement without an order number, so he said he would ask his supervisor to deal with the query, but the supervisor was on another call, would I like to hold? Definitely not. I rang off with the promise that the supervisor would call back very soon. The supervisor did not call back that day and I was annoyed. So I telephoned the next day and told them forcibly that their service left a lot to be desired. The customer service agent who answered must have had a bad day, because he was rude and unhelpful; this made me even angrier and we finished shouting at each other down the telephone.

Five minutes later a supervisor called me back to apologize and explain that the agent who had taken his call had a bad cold and was not feeling very well. He said he would authorize a replacement keyboard straightaway, but first the company needed the faulty keyboard returned to their warehouse. The supervisor arranged for a special collection as a way of making amends, but forgot to ask me for the original order number. The keyboard was duly collected, but as there was no order number it did not get checked into the depot in the usual way.

Three days went by and no keyboard. I telephoned again to find out what had happened and found that as the company had no record of receiving the keyboard back, no replacement had been sent out. I told them in no uncertain terms that this was their problem and not mine. They could not find a way out of their self-imposed bind, so I asked for (and got) a refund and bought a keyboard from another company. A whole week was wasted. I have not used the company again.

Suppose you were the customer service manager charged with sorting out this mess and making sure it did not happen again. What questions would you ask?

'What happened?'
This would be a good start. Look at the immediate system without judgement – the customer, the supervisor, the customer service representative and the warehouse. Finding out exactly what happened might actually be difficult, however, because people edit their accounts to put themselves in the best light, in case they get the blame. They tell you their intentions, not necessarily the straight facts.
'Who's to blame?'
This is the least helpful question, as it just rakes over the past.
'Was it the customer's fault for being so unpleasant?'
In his mind, he had very good reasons, he was frustrated, could not do his work, had a deadline to make and was exasperated at what he saw as a lack of professionalism.
'Was it the supervisor's fault for not calling back initially?'
He was overworked.
'Should the courier should have checked the parcel and asked for the order number?'
But that wasn't his job.
'Was the customer service representative to blame for losing his temper?'
But he had a cold.
'Was it the fault of the cold virus?!'
The virus could claim it was only doing what it was built to do...

Blame evolution.
We need not pursue this – blame leads nowhere and every-where. It is actually possible to blame anyone in a system, because everyone is part of it. But blame takes you into the

past, does nothing to ensure the future and usually makes individuals feel even less resourceful. It looks at events, not the patterns behind them.

A leader's questions would be:

How did we make ourselves vulnerable to this situation?
How can we change what we do so it does not happen
  again?

Any disaster can be valuable, if you learn from it. People make mistakes, to err is human, but is to forgive company policy?

Mistakes are feedback that can improve the whole organization. Also, how the leader deals with them gives a good measure of their skills.

Of course it may be true that some people are not up to the job, in which case the team leader should ask themselves whether they have an adequate recruitment procedure, or whether the job has been made too difficult.

To go back to my example, there are many other questions that would uncover how the system did not deliver the results it was designed for:

Have there been other instances like this in the recent
  past?
What do they have in common?
Do recruitment procedures need to be changed?
Is customer service training adequate?
How well supported are customer service people?
Are they given sufficient responsibility to deal with
  problems without having to call in the supervisor?
Is the supervisor overworked because he is always being
  called to deal with petty matters?
Should we overhaul the warehouse procedure for receiving
  faulty parts?

These question procedures, but every business procedure is based on an idea, a belief or a mental model of how things

are. When we shift to thinking about the mental models behind the procedures, we open up a whole new set of
questions. For example:

What level of decision can customer support be trusted to
    take without supervision?
Are customers trustworthy?
Are they trying to get something for nothing?

Mental models can be uncovered by the question 'Why?', if
you ask it persistently enough. Keep asking until you get answers that go beyond blaming individuals.

Why did the customer lose his temper?
Because he was not called back as promised.
Why?
Because the supervisor was overworked.
Why?
Because his staff were not authorized to take certain
    decisions on their own.

Keep asking 'Why?' until you see how the system is responsible for what has happened.

The structure of any organization is kept intact by its procedures and these are the result of certain ways of thinking.
Leaders have to change these ways of thinking – unless they
change the mental models behind the procedures, another
procedure that accomplishes the same purpose will simply
grow in its place. It's like the mythological Hydra – if you
keep cutting off the head, two more grow in its place. You
have to get to the heart of the beast, the point in the system
where change will make a difference – the leverage point.
This nearly always involves changing people's ideas, beliefs,
attitudes and mental models.

Changing mental models is generative learning, so it fol-
lows that if the model is changed, then the procedures will
change too. Change a procedure without changing the mental models, on the other hand, and the new way will be

forced into service of the old idea and will not work as intended.

Blame does have some useful function: it channels feelings. When we blame someone it gives us a release for our anger and frustrations. Systems do not have feelings, but people do, and blaming individuals and getting angry with them at least offers an outlet for those feelings. I was angry with the computer supply firm for making a mess of my order. I lost time. I felt aggrieved. This shouldn't have happened! The feelings of everyone were very real. How do you deal with these feelings? Systems thinking is fine, but there is also systems *feeling*.

You may not be able to blame anyone in the system, but that does not mean that no one is responsible. Here is the paradox. People may be doing the best they can given the system they are in, but they may still make mistakes, and you may be seriously hurt or inconvenienced by their mistakes or the way the system operates. Seeing how systems work does not excuse or condone injustice and suffering, poor practice, inefficiency or complacency, and the feelings these evoke in us are authentic and important. Whether we find ourselves part of such systems or on the receiving end of them, when we understand how they operate, we have a choice of what to do and more possibilities for change. Also, understanding how systems work saves us from some of life's petty annoyances.

People in a system are still responsible for doing the best they can to make it work as well as possible if it is a just one and to change it if it is an unjust one. Leaders do feel strongly, sometimes strongly enough to challenge governments. They hold people responsible and they accept responsibility themselves for their part in the system.

My friend's daughter was bullied by a classmate at primary school. She became afraid to go to school. My friend and his wife went several times to complain to the class teacher and to the head teacher, but despite this, the bullying continued in covert ways. My friend became very angry. His main feeling and responsibility was as a parent to his young daughter.

Yes, the school was doing its best, yes, teachers were doing their best. His daughter was coping with it as best she could. But nothing was changing and the situation was intolerable. So he took his daughter away from that school. He held the school responsible but not to blame for the situation.

Systems can be infuriating. Procedures which have the intention of making things easy can be used to frustrate and limit us. Everyone has their horror story about the perils of bureaucracy. Systems may work in an impersonal way, but in the end, people are responsible for making them work the way they do. The paradox is that the focus of your feeling, the hapless person who fills a place in the system, can probably do little to change it. Understanding the way systems work can make sure that the energy and feeling you have can be directed to the right place to change the system.

Change and Balance

The leader's work is change and there are two sorts of change. The first is change *in* the system – the kind of change you need to make to stay the same. This is like keeping your balance. Balance does not mean trying to keep absolutely still and rigid, if you did, you would topple over. Balance means always making small adjustments, changing your position slightly all the time. Your body, for instance, may seem the same, but it is constantly renewing itself. A year from now, over 90 per cent of the atoms in your body will be different. In business, people leave, new people arrive, a company shifts and changes, yet in some way it is still the same company. The longer it has been established, the more it will have changed, yet paradoxically, the more stable it will appear. Change gives stability.

The other kind of change is change *of* the system. This second order change means finding a new balance point, and involves deeper and wider change. An organization needs to change to survive; it needs to evolve and adapt to the changing market. This change may be gradual or drastic.

Where does a business set its point of stability? With any change it is just as important to know what to keep the same, what core processes to organize around, as it is to know what to change. Here a leader has the role of a steward. There are four fundamental questions any company needs to answer:

- What is our purpose? What are we trying to accomplish?
- How do we stay competitive in the market?
- How do we deliver a high performance?
- How do we cope with change?

The answers to these questions are what a business has to self-organize around. A business needs the stability that fixed procedures bring, but enough room for creativity and innovation to keep it alive and balanced. How much of each is right?

Scylla and Charybdis

There are two great dangers for leaders while navigating the dangerous waters of a rapidly changing market. On one hand there stands the dead weight of too much procedure and not enough flexibility. Such a business cannot respond to outside changes quickly enough. This does not depend on the size of the company (Microsoft, a huge company by any standard, turned around its Internet policy inside six months in 1996), but on how much the company is governed by fixed policy and procedures.

The second danger comes from the opposite direction – too much innovation and change. Such a business is chaotic, the employees are confused and disorientated. What they do and how they do it changes too rapidly, as the business heads for the equivalent of a nervous breakdown.

These two dangers are like monsters ready to swallow and destroy an organization. In Greek mythology Scylla and Charybdis were two sea monsters that lived on either side of a narrow strait. A ship had to brave the dangerous passage, there was no way around. Scylla had six long necks, each with a head with three rows of teeth. Any sailors that came within reach of the heads were snapped up and devoured. The monster was always in motion, weaving backwards and forwards, the heads yapping at the passing sailors. Charybdis was quieter, but just as deadly. It made a whirlpool that sucked in water three times a day and then let it out in a huge spout, destroying any ship within range. In business, a leader must not only navigate all the ordinary dangers of the market (the rocks and tides), but also avoid falling into the chaos of Scylla or the petrified inactivity of Charybdis.

Generally companies tend to favour the side of Charybdis and confuse stability with rigidity. They are not stable but pseudo-stable, and may be increasingly out of date, bearing in mind that the procedures they may be clinging to will have been set up to solve the problems of yesterday. Many firms have ways of damping down changes that undermine the existing order. But the best way to deal with change and uncertainty is not to try to resist it but to move with it. When a business resists change, or tries to push it to the margins, the pressure may build up and lead to a sudden drastic upheaval. Politics shows this most clearly. The East German Communist regime spent close to 50 years trying to prevent change. When it did come it was sudden, violent and unstoppable. The longer you put off changing, the deeper it will be when it comes. The more you suppress it, the more violent it will be.

Normal, internally driven change that keeps a company stable tends to follow a pattern.

First, there is a space for people to innovate, to vary procedures, to experiment and try out different solutions. There is flexibility in the procedures, a variety of informal channels, rules that can be bent and broken. This is not the same as having a research department for new products, it means renewing the company from the inside in small ways. Informal channels where people share information and make connections will not undermine existing processes but lead to innovation and renewal. Informal channels that grow to bypass inadequate formal processes do not lead to renewal but to cover up and confusion. They only hide the problem. The informal connections have to be open and recognized as valuable. Does the business culture encourage this?

Secondly, the innovation gains ground because it is useful, seen as a possible answer to a problem in another part of the company. It may get a sponsor.

Lastly, the new idea becomes more solid, people work on it and it may be made into a procedure or a product that is marketed internally or externally.

When this three-part cycle is allowed to happen it keeps the company healthy. Ninety per cent of these new ideas may come to nothing, but one of the other 10 per cent could become the core product or service in five years' time. It is important to explore avenues even when they do not seem very promising at first glance.

What is the leader's role in this process? Maybe as the innovator of the idea. Perhaps as the sponsor. Certainly as a force in creating a culture where innovation and difference can flower.

The whole process is like evolution in the biological world. Nature continually innovates, creating both different forms and variations of the same form. No two animals are alike in the same species. The differences may be slight, but if they give an advantage in the environment over time, they will survive and be transmitted and eventually give rise to a whole new species or genus. This organic metaphor appeals to me more than a machine metaphor like re-engineering. I also think it is more accurate. The word 'organization' has the same root as 'organic', and 'organism', meaning a whole living system. The root of the word 'corporation' is the Latin word *corporis*, meaning a living body. Leaders keep an organization alive and healthy.

We cannot predict the future, but innovation is the way to adapt in advance. Continual innovation primes a company for many possible futures. Any company that rests on its laurels will have them stolen. A business is either on the way up or on the way down. The moment you have reached a peak, you start to slip down the other side. Business continually seeks different peaks to climb. The dangers are that what seems like a peak is a foothill, or, worse, that all the competitors are climbing a different mountain range. Excellence is not enough; it is too static a concept. The hot companies of today can turn into the cold turkeys of tomorrow.

In Search of Excellence by Peters and Waterman[3] was the business bestseller of 1982. It told the stories of the most successful businesses of the time. However, it modelled the excellent businesses of the late 1970s. They were not necessarily adapted to the 1980s. Three years after the book was published only a minority of those excellent businesses was still excellent by the same criteria. In the 1990s the focus is on change, the response is innovation and the prize is sustainability. The new business bestseller could be called 'In Search of Sustainability'.

The Edge of Chaos

The place of balance between the Scylla of too much freedom and the Charybdis of too much order is known in complexity theory as the edge of chaos. Here there is enough freedom to continually evolve and change, and enough structure to stay stable and function well. The stability and order give the business continuity, efficiency, planning and some degree of control. The freedom means there is room for creativity, variety, risk taking, experimentation and entrepreneurship. The edge of chaos is where an organization can learn.

Much of the time we tiptoe up to this edge, take one look into the teeming depths below and draw back sharply in favour of habit, comfort and conformity. Yet this is the best place to be. An organization needs to be able to meet and adapt to the changing environment, and the more the environment changes, the more flexible the organization needs to be. The edge of chaos is that rare combination where freedom balances structure. Also, at the edge of chaos, an organization is most effective at turning data into information, and information into knowledge, because it has the structure to collect the information and the internal connections and creativity to put it together to generate knowledge, value, insight and foresight.

Can a business reach this magical point on its own? Not without a leader to take it there. A leader must create a culture that encourages risk taking, creativity and uniqueness within a pattern of continuity and order, a culture that is not maintained by rules, penalties and rigid boundaries, but by values and vision, trust and commitment. There is no recipe for getting to the edge; every company is different, needing different degrees of freedom and order depending on what it does and how it is structured. There are some broad guiding principles, however.

The degree of communication within a company is important. How well do people communicate and connect? When connections are too thin, then the organization is too rigid, it cannot react quickly enough. Too many connections and it becomes chaotic – a change in one part re-echoes throughout and disturbs the whole system, making it impossible to work. It is like a precariously balanced house of cards – tip one and they all fall over. Each part of the business needs some autonomy. When parts of the organization are too enmeshed, each part must have some freedom of action otherwise it will always be reacting to changes in other departments. Some changes need to be transmitted, but not all.

One way that organizations become too rigid is by trying to cover all eventualities, to make procedures fail-safe. You can never make a complex system fail-safe, it is impossible to control everything and attempts to do so make for too many rigid rules. It seems what can go wrong, will go wrong ... eventually. Industrial disasters happen despite the most elaborate safety precautions. Take a tip from nature. Your body is not designed so that it can never go wrong; it is not fail-safe. It is designed so that if it does go wrong the damage is minimised and localized; it is designed to be safe-fail.

A balance of freedom and order means giving people responsibility for their work and not trying to control them or making rules to cover every eventuality. A manager who makes a lot of easy decisions every day about what people should do is doing too much controlling. The more command and control, the less possibility of inspiring leadership.

The edge of chaos is where the *whole* organization needs to be, so some parts of the business may be more structured than others. For example, the accounts department will need more structure than marketing, manufacturing more than research and development, yet the totals will balance overall.

I saw a very interesting piece about some ongoing research that seems to validate these ideas. Eliot Maltz, Assistant Professor of Marketing at the University of Southern California, and Ajay Kohli, Professor of Marketing at the University of Texas,[4] carried out a study of 788 managers from manufacturing, research and development and finance departments in 265 high-technology companies. They looked at how well the marketing departments were able to communicate their ideas to other departments. The number of contacts was crucial. When the marketing managers had fewer than 10 contacts a week, their information was not used well by the other departments, and the marketing managers did not understand how to give the right sort of information at the right time and in the right way. Too few contacts did not communicate the information in the best way. So were more contacts better? Yes – but only up to a point. Results were good from 10 to 25 contacts a week, then the effect levelled off. The research also showed that if the marketing managers communicated with their colleagues in other departments more than 40 times a week they ran the risk of having their work undervalued and subsequently ignored. Too much communication is just as bad as too little. The research also found that 50 per cent of the non-marketing managers felt that they had too little information from their marketing colleagues and only 5 per cent felt they got too much, which shows a bias towards too little contact.

The contacts could be formal or informal – fax, e-mail, memo or even an informal chat over coffee. The best mixture of communication in the crucial 25–40 band was an equal mixture of formal and informal communication. Formal communication was the official channels, giving the bare information; the informal contacts were just as important to give the context, the people's feelings and subjective analysis of the information, and often reasons and explanations that could not go into the written and publicly available report. Managers needed both parts of the message to make the best sense of the situation, both the bare official bones and the rich human context in which they were embedded. Also, the informal meetings allowed the other managers to ask questions to clarify the official information and apply it better to their situation.

I find this research very suggestive. It shows the edge-of-chaos effect in just one small part of an organization.

The Power Law

How much should an organization change? How often? Complexity theory has some interesting suggestions. A complex system is at the edge of chaos when there is a relationship between the rate of change and the size of the change. This relationship is called a 'power law'. Changes follow a power law when the average frequency of a change is inversely proportional to some power of its size – in other words, many small changes but very few large ones.

The power law is very common in nature. It is seen in the behaviour of light from the sun, sunspots, the flow of water in a river, and in the size and frequency of earthquakes. Large tremors are rare, but there are many small tremors. Stock prices and traffic flows in a city also follow a power law.

The Danish physicist Per Bak uses an excellent metaphor to explain how a power law applies to a system in a critical state.[5] Imagine sand raining down into a pile until it is just balanced and cannot grow any higher. It is just stable, the balance seems precarious but no grains are slipping. Now let another grain of sand hit the pile. We do not know what will happen. Perhaps nothing. Perhaps a few grains will be disturbed. Perhaps a chain reaction will be set off that leads to the collapse of the pile into another heap that is just balanced. You cannot predict exactly what will happen, but most of the time there will be a small avalanche. Very occasionally there will be a large one.

Any system poised at the edge of chaos will show changes that follow a power law. I think this is an evocative and suggestive metaphor for organizations and individuals. Look back to the figure on page 174. A power law means that there should be very many shallow and narrow changes in sector 1 of the graph, fewer in sector 2 and 3 and very few wide and deep changes in sector 4. This rate of change makes the company not just adaptive but sustainable.

Leaders must be able to create change – both to change the organization and to keep it in balance.

Chaos		Order
	Edge of chaos	

Too little procedure	Sustainability	Too much procedure
Anarchy	Knowledge	Too many rules
Confusion	Learning	Rigidity
Risk taking		No risk
Too many connections		Too few connections
Free for all		Command and control
Informal rather than formal contacts		Formal rather than informal contacts
Gossip		Isolation

Our lives are as complex as any organization, although in a different way, and I think it is very interesting to apply these metaphors to our personal lives as well. Let us speculate that perhaps we too need to change and renew ourselves. We too need to find a balance between structure and creativity, we too need to sail the straits between a life too mired in habit, which is the personal equivalent of organizational procedure, and one that is too chaotic to give us the chance to express ourselves fully.

The Flow State of creativity and ease may be the individual equivalent of the edge of chaos. The Flow State has been described as one of 'alert and effortless control', one of 'active relaxation'.[6] For the body, health and well-being are the equivalent of the edge of chaos. Here too we need to find a balance between trust and rules, between formal and informal communication. We know that a lack of social contact is bad for our health – perhaps it is also possible to lose ourselves in too much social contact. And how well and how often do we communicate with ourselves on the inside? How well do we know ourselves? What do we organize ourselves around? What are we drawn towards?

For a leader it is a vision.

Individual

Chaos		Order
	Flow	
Anxiety	Edge of chaos	Habit
Confusion		Rigidity
Disorder		Fixed routine
Inability to concentrate		Boredom
		Obsessional behaviour

I am fascinated to see if and how the edge of chaos and the power law idea might apply to the changes we make in our lives. Delve into the metaphor a little. Here is an exercise you can use to explore and speculate.

Take a time in your life, say the last one or two years, and make a list of all the changes that have happened. Place them in approximate order, from the ones that affected you the most and you feel most strongly about down to the very minor everyday ones.

Give them a measurement as happens when finding a person's stress level, but this is not about stress. The figure you give each is completely up to you – perhaps 100 for the most significant change, down to 1 for the minor ones.

Now put them on a grid as shown in the diagram.

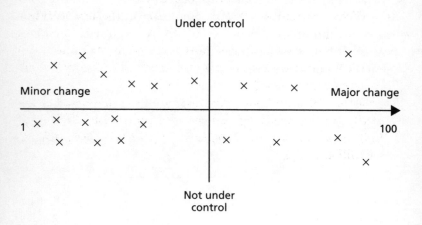

What patterns can you see?

Do you need to make more changes or fewer changes in your life?

How many of the large changes were your choice?

References

1 First, second and third perceptual positions were developed by John Grinder and Judith DeLozier in their book *Turtles All the Way Down*, Grinder DeLozier and Associates, 1987, republished by Metamorphous Press in 1994.

   The English biologist and systems thinker Gregory Bateson carried out the original work on perceptual positions. See his *Steps to an Ecology of Mind*, Jason Aronsen, 1987.

2 See Alexandre de Faria, *Quality Management of Development Co-operation. Volume II: The Methods*, UNIDO.

3 T. Peters and H. Waterman, *In Search of Excellence*, Macmillan, 1982

4 See *Harvard Business Review*, January–February 1998, page 10.

5 See Per Bak and Chen Kan, 'Self-organized criticality', *Scientific American*, January 1991, pp.46–53.

6 See Mihaly Csikszentmihalyi, *Flow: The Psychology of Happiness*, Rider, 1992.

   For a detailed introduction to systems thinking see Joseph O'Connor and Ian McDermott, *The Art of Systems Thinking*, Thorsons, 1997.

   For an excellent introduction to the science of complexity see M. Waldrop, *Complexity*, Simon and Schuster, 1993, or Roger Lewin, *Complexity: Life at the Edge of Chaos*, Macmillan, 1992.

8

CONCLUSION

In a traditional adventure story, the hero returns to take up his life again, but it is a different life, because he is a different person; his adventure has changed him. Life is not so neatly parcelled out as in stories and the end of one story is the beginning of the next. There is no point at which you can sit back metaphorically on your laurels and think, 'That's it. I'm a leader. Now I can relax.'

Leadership is often presented as a package – do all these things and you will become a leader. The package is attractive from the outside, but I hope we have got beyond the wrapping to what being a leader means to you, so you can develop your own style of leadership and be a leader in your own way, a way that fits with your own ethical and moral sense. Being a leader starts with being yourself.

I think of leadership as a general set of skills, values and a way of being that you can apply anywhere, in family life, in work, whatever you do. Although much of this book has concentrated on leadership in business, because this is a particularly important application, I have aimed to put some of the skills of business leadership into a wider context because I do not believe you can separate the business leader from the person. The way to transform a company begins with transforming yourself and becoming a leader is one way to transform yourself. I also believe that for every obstacle we meet in the outside world and every problem we solve there we have to overcome an inner obstacle and solve an inner problem.

A leader's vision takes them into the future and the future is an adventure. The very word 'adventure' means 'going out'. Leadership is an adventure of self-development, of finding resources to overcome the setbacks and the guardians on the way. And it is an adventure of going outside yourself, overcoming external obstacles, developing your companions and achieving your vision.

Obstacles and resistance are not always what they seem. Japanese temples are often guarded by statues that look like ferocious demons. The first thing you notice about them is one hand held up in a stern gesture with the palm outward. It clearly means 'STOP!' But when you look more closely, you see the other hand is making an inviting gesture for you to enter. What is the real message? It is whichever one you pay attention to.

Traditionally, a leader cannot move on to the next stage of their adventure until they have found someone to replace them at the level they were on. So leadership is also about being a coach, a mentor and developing others as leaders.

Of the many skills and ideas in this book, three stand out for me. First is building trust – trust in yourself and trust in others. Trust is built first of all by pacing, understanding where you are right now and acknowledging that. Then you build trust by continually testing your own strength and that of others. You can only do that by co-operating, by assuming at least at the start that others are trustworthy. This also links to optimism. Leaders assume they will succeed unless they have evidence to the contrary. They do not assume they will fail. At the same time, however, they look very carefully at all the difficulties that could stand in the way and plan for them.

Take a moment now to review your own ideas on leadership.

What is it about leadership that has made the most impression on you?
What ideas about leadership are you most attracted to?
What ideas are you least attracted to?
What ideas about leadership have you had confirmed?

What new ideas have you gained?
To which area are you drawn as a leader?

What is the most uncertain, even risky, situation in
   your life at the moment?
That's precisely the place where you have the best
   opportunity to be a leader.

The second idea that stands out for me is generative learning – continually questioning your assumptions. We build a business, even a life, based on our beliefs and assumptions. Then we do not distinguish between those beliefs that are important to us and empowering and those that are not.

What would it be like if you were to put your belief system on the edge of chaos? This sounds an alarming metaphor, but consider. You would be constantly examining and being open to changing your beliefs in small ways that would best help you towards your vision. Occasionally, you would make a large change, but all the changes would keep you open to new experience. By keeping your belief system alive in this way, you might not have an unexpected and unwelcome surprise when an important assumption turns out to be misleading.

Belief systems are not formed once and for all, we all have a museum of old beliefs, and the exhibits are out-of-date beliefs that we have disproved, or just outgrown.

The third important idea is balancing change and order. Leaders create change, but against a backdrop of stability. There is one more ingredient to successful change – good timing. Try for a change too soon and the status quo will be too strong, too late and the moment will have passed. Something else will be needed.

How do you know the right time to make your move? You don't. You have to trust. Sometimes you can sense where people want to go and move with them. The good leader knows where people want to go and gets out in front. When you are in tune with events, your timing will always be right. I think timing is partly aesthetic. We all have an aesthetic sense, a sense of rightness, of beauty and proportion. We sense when events come together and it is time for something new to happen. Again, we have to trust that aesthetic sense. It is like listening to music or telling a good story. Some stories ring true, others do not. Good stories set up expectations, they are satisfying, and there is a balance between action and reflection that is aesthetically pleasing.[1]

A vision is what inspires you, it drives the plot of the story, but it must stay open to feedback. Values also need to be open to feedback. Leaders may fall into the trap of fanaticism when they take values to extremes. Every political leader comes to power on a vision of sorts, underpinned by values. Yet any value loses its 'value' when it is pursued to the extreme. In this case more is not better.

We have already talked a lot about the value of change as against the value of order. Either one taken to the limit can undermine you. There are other examples. Individuality is a good value to have and so is a belief in the importance of relationships. Pursuing either to the limit, though, would not be healthy. The same goes for task and relationship, and complete trust or complete mistrust. Keeping a balance of values, especially those that are the most important to you, keeps you out of the trap of thinking you know what is best for others and forcing your solutions on them.[2]

The Paradox of Values

Think of a value that is very important to you, either in your personal life or in the business organization where you work. Ask yourself some questions to explore the limit of this value:

What vision is this value in the service of?

What is it a guiding principle for?

How does it help me towards my vision?

How might it hinder me if I took it to extremes?

What is the opposite value that would balance this value and also perhaps be a guiding principle towards my vision?

How could this value help me?

How could it hinder me if I took it to extremes?

What would happen if I allowed the first value to dominate the second, balancing value?

What would happen if I allowed the balancing value to dominate the first?

At what point would each value start to undermine its opposite?

How would I know if this were to happen?

Remember the starlings, flying in formation, somehow staying together and keeping their alignment without any single bird as permanent leader? Researchers have been able to simulate flocking behaviour on a computer by making the birds follow three simple rules. First each bird must maintain a minimum distance from others. In other words, the relationships between the birds is important – not too near and not too far. Secondly, each bird must try to match velocity with those around it. So everyone moves at the same pace. Thirdly, each bird should try to move towards the perceived centre of the mass of birds in its neighbourhood.

We know that very complex behaviour can be built up from very simple rules. The intricate pattern of flocking emerges out of simple rules operating at the individual level, but the rules are about the individual's relationship to the whole group. When migratory birds fly together no one bird could reach its destination on its own. The birds need each other. When the leader tires, it drops back and flies behind, supported by other birds. I wonder what simple rules apply to an aligned team, each person capable of being a leader, each supporting the others when necessary, each being able to take over a leadership role, and all heading for the same destination. I suspect they may be to do with trust, balance of change and making the right sort of connections.

Finally, a leader inspires action. Vision without action is impotent, just as action without vision is meaningless. The two greatest orators in ancient Greece were Socrates and Demosthenes. Both men spoke to the assembled army before a battle and urged them to move against their enemies.

First Socrates made his speech. The listeners cheered and shouted, 'That was a great speech!'

Then Demosthenes spoke. When he had finished, there was a hush. Then the army shouted, 'Let us march!' Demosthenes was more of the leader here.

We are all moving towards some vision, whatever we call it and however we think about it. *Bon voyage* and good companionship.

References

1 See Nelson Zink and Joe Munshaw, 'Elements of syntactic awareness', *Anchor Point*, June 1997, page 13.
2 See Charles Hampden-Turner and Alfons Trompenaars, *The Seven Cultures of Capitalism*, Macmillan, 1994.

RESOURCES

Training and Consultancy

Lambent Training offers consultancy and training based on Neuro Linguistic Programming and systems thinking.

We use systems thinking and complexity in our consultancy for:
* high performance
* developing business strategy
* knowledge management

We use NLP for developing people, improving individual skills through coaching and training, and team building meetings.

We design training in-house for business and also offer three training seminars that can be tailored to individual businesses:

Leadership: The Leader's Journey
The training based on this book:
high performance through leadership
developing your leadership skills
communication skills – influencing others
systemic thinking skills

Systems Thinking in Business
working with mental models in the organization
single and double loop learning – changing the thinking that
    gave rise to the problem
dealing with organizational inertia to change
working with feedback and dealing with time delays
recognizing systems archetypes and patterns

NLP for Business
using NLP in business for coaching, training and development
aligning personal and organizational values and goals
working styles
team building

Systems Thinking Certification Training
This five-day public training covers:
the basics of systems in a practical way
understanding the effects of feedback
complexity
time delays
mental models
systems archetypes

For details of all training and consultancy contact:
Lambent Training
4 Coombe Gardens
New Malden
Surrey
KT3 4AA
UK

Tel: +44 (0)181 715 2560
Fax: +44 (0)181 715 2560
Website: www.lambent.com

BIBLIOGRAPHY

Adair, John, *Effective Leadership*, Pan, 1983

Aryris, Chris, *Overcoming Organizational Defences*, Prentice-Hall, 1990

Bandler, Richard, *Using your Brain for a Change*, Real People Press, 1985

Bateson, Gregory, *Mind and Nature*, Fontana, 1980

Bateson, Gregory, *Steps to an Ecology of Mind*, Jason Arenson, 1987

Bennis, Warren, *On Becoming a Leader*, Hutchinson, 1990

Block, Peter, *Stewardship*, Berrett-Koehler, 1996

Brown, Shona, and Eisenhardt, Kathleen, *Competing on the Edge: Strategy as Structured Chaos*, Harvard Business School Publishing, 1998

Capra Fritjof, *The Web of Life*, Flamingo, 1997

Carlton, Jim, *Apple: The Inside Story of Intrigue, Egomania and Business Blunders*, Times Books, 1997

Courtney, Hugh, Kirkland, Janet, and Viguerie, Patrick, 'Strategy under uncertainty', *Harvard Business Review*, November–December 1977

Csikszentmihalyi, Mihaly, *Flow: The Psychology of Happiness*, Rider, 1992

Dilts, Robert, *Skills for the Future*, Meta Publications, 1993

Drucker, Peter, *The New Realities*, Heinemann, 1989

Fritz, R., *The Path of Least Resistance*, Ballantine, 1989

Gardner, John, W., *On Leadership*, Free Press, 1989

Gleick, James, *Chaos: Making of a New Science*, Viking, 1987

Handy, Charles, *The Empty Raincoat*, Hutchinson, 1994

Kelly, Kevin, *Out of Control*, Fourth Estate, 1994

Kohn, Alfie, *Punished by Rewards*, Houghton Mifflin, 1993

Kotter, John, *The Leadership Factor*, Free Press, 1988

Lewin, Roger, *Complexity*, Macmillan, 1992

Liberating Leadership, The Industrial Society, 1997

McDermott, Ian, and O'Connor, Joseph, *Practical NLP for Managers* Gower, 1996

Machiavelli, N., *The Prince*, Penguin, 1961

The Management Agenda, Roffey Park, 1998

Mintzberg, Henry, *Mintzberg on Management*, Macmillan, 1989

Mitroff, Ian and Linstone, Harold, *The Unbounded Mind*, Oxford University Press, 1993

O'Connor, Joseph, and McDermott, Ian, *The Art of Systems Thinking* Thorsons, 1997

O'Connor, Joseph, McDermott, Ian, and Prior, Robin, *Practical NLP for Managers Workbook*, Gower, 1996

O'Connor, Joseph, and Seymour, John, *Introducing NLP*, Thorsons, 1995

Pascale, Richard, Millemann, Mark, and Goija, Linda, 'Changing the way we change', *Harvard Business Review*, November–December 1977

Prigogone, Ilya, *Order Out of Chaos*, Bantam, 1984

Sabanci, Sapik, *This is My Life*, World of Information, 1988

Senge, Peter, *The Fifth Discipline*, Doubleday, 1990

Senge, Peter *et al.*, *The Fifth Discipline Fieldbook*, Doubleday, 1990

Sun Tzu, *The Art of War*, Delacorte Press, 1983

Waldrop, M., *Complexity*, Simon and Schuster, 1993

Wheatley, Margaret J., *Leadership and the New Science*, Berrett-Koehler, 1992

About the Author

Joseph O'Connor is a leading author, trainer and consultant in the field of leadership, systems thinking and personal development. He is a certified trainer in Neuro-Linguistic Programming (NLP).

Joseph gives training on NLP, systems thinking and leadership in Europe, Asia and America. Corporate clients include UNIDO, BA, BT, Hewlett-Packard and ICI. He has a BSc in anthropology from London University and is a Licentiate of the Royal College of Music. His background in music and the performing arts has resulted in research into musical skills and acting skills in the theatre.

This book on leadership brings together many of the strands that have interested him over the years: self-development, values and the relationships we create with one another, both directly and through the systems we make.

He is also fascinated by the new technology of communications and is a founder of a company that designs interactive psychological software for business and home use.

Joseph's bestselling book *Introducing NLP*, written with John Seymour, is now established as the basic introductory text in Neuro-Linguistic Programming and has been translated into 14 languages. Some of his other books have also been published in several languages.

Other books:

Not Pulling Strings, Lambent Books, 1987

Introducing Neuro-Linguistic Programming (with John Seymour), Thorsons, 1990

Training with NLP (with John Seymour), Thorsons, 1994

Successful Selling with NLP (with Robin Prior), Thorsons, 1995
Principles of NLP (with Ian McDermott), Thorsons, 1996
Practical NLP for Managers (with Ian McDermott), Gower, 1996
NLP and Health (with Ian McDermott), Thorsons, 1996
The Art of Systems Thinking (with Ian McDermott), Thorsons, 1997

Audiotapes:

An Introduction to NLP (with Ian McDermott), Thorsons, 1997
NLP, Health and Well-being (with Ian McDermott), Thorsons, 1998
Leading with NLP, Thorsons, 1998

Contact Joseph:
c/o Lambent Training
4 Coombe Gardens
New Malden
Surrey
KT3 4AA
UK

Telephone and fax: +44 (0)181 715 2560
E-mail: lambent@well.com

INDEX

THE ART OF SYSTEMS THINKING

Essential skills for creativity and problem solving

Joseph O'Connor & Ian McDermott

Systems thinking goes beyond logic, because people are not always logical. Systems thinking sees beyond isolated events to the deeper patterns and connections.

This is important, because we live in a world of systems. Your body is a system, so is your family. The natural environment is a system, as is your business. Understanding how these systems work will dramatically increase your effectiveness, save you time and help you to achieve your goals.

Systems thinking is practical and immensely useful. It is not an academic discipline requiring mathematics or engineering to understand it. This book explains the principles of systems thinking in a straightforward way with practical applications, exercises and examples that will help you become more influential and successful in managing your health, work, finances and relationships.

Joseph O'Connor is a trainer, consultant and author of many books on psychology and communication skills, including the bestselling *Introducing NLP*.

Ian McDermott is Director of Training for International Teaching Seminars, a leading NLP training organisation in the UK.

NLP AND HEALTH

Ian McDermott & Joseph O'Connor

We create our own health – by what we do, how we think, how we live. Our bodies metabolize not just food and air, but all our experiences too; they respond to the world we create in our minds. NLP (Neuro-Linguistic Programming) studies the way our thoughts affect our wellbeing. *NLP and Health* brings together the latest medical research, and your experience of your own health in a practical way, by revealing:

- how we create our internal world and how our bodies respond with either health or illness
- how our emotional state affects our immune system and what we can do about this
- remarkable recoveries from terminal illness – and what they teach us about health
- the different ways we think about health and their consequences
- how the way you think can be one of the most accurate predictors of how long you will live
- how stress and worry build up, how to deal with them, and how to use your senses to gain pleasure and enhance your mental power
- why being ill does not always mean you are unhealthy

This book is for you if you seek health and well-being and would like to find out how NLP works, if you are looking for practical ways in which your mind and body can work in harmony, if you believe there is more to health than not being ill and if you want to find out more about that most fascinating of enigmas – yourself.

PRINCIPLES OF NLP

Joseph O'Connor & Ian McDermott

Neuro-Linguistic Programming (NLP) is the psychology of excellence. It is based on the practical skills that are used by all good communicators to obtain excellent results. These skills are invaluable for personal and professional development. This introductory guide explains:

- what NLP is
- how to use it in your life personally, spiritually and professionally
- how to understand body language
- how to achieve excellence in everything that you do

LEADING WITH NLP

Essential leadership skills for influencing and managing people

Joseph O'Connor

Why be a leader? To be involved in what really matters to you. To be able to do what is important to you with others who share your passion.

Leadership is a natural part of life, a skill that can be learned, not a magical quality you are born with. It does not depend on high profile and glamour. It is an essential skill in modern business.

Start your journey now towards developing your own style of leadership.

Beyond management – to inspiration. Leaders make the difference in business through high performance and innovation.

Beyond influence – to choice. Leaders motivate others through a shared vision and values.

Beyond authority – to trust. Leadership gives a natural strength that comes from who you are.

Leading with NLP tells you how to:

- develop and use your own natural leadership style
- create shared vision
- use strategic thinking
- create trust
- overcome resistance and reluctance to move forward.

You cannot be a leader on your own. Others make you a leader. *Leading with NLP* is about the beliefs and actions that will make you a leader for yourself and others, and gives practical ways to develop the skills you need.

Also available in audio.

SUCCESSFUL SELLING WITH NLP

Neuro-linguistic programming, the way forward in the New Bazaar

Joseph O'Connor and Robin Prior

Are you caught in the Old Bazaar?
Where selling is seen as manipulative?
Where sales people are not highly valued?
Where the motto is: 'Let the buyer beware?'

Are you threatened by the Electronic Bazaar?
Where technology rather than the salesperson is used to match customer and product?
Where consumer groups and legislation are increasingly having an impact?
Where the motto is: 'Let the salesperson beware?'

Sales is changing under these two pressures to a new model – The New Bazaar. This is a new sales culture dominated by relationship, integrity and influence for a win-win result. NLP is the study of how we communicate with each other and offers powerful ways for sales people and customers to get what they want in the New Bazaar.

If you are a salesperson, sales manager, or a professional who needs skill to sell your product or service, this book is invaluable.

TRAINING WITH NLP

Neuro-linguistic programming skills for managers, trainers and communicators

Joseph O'Connor & John Seymour

Training is already a £3 billion per year business in the UK. Changes in technology and organisational development make it likely that 75 per cent of people working today are likely to need training within the next 10 years. Training can be one of the most effective ways to learn the new skills and knowledge needed for the future. The opportunities for outstanding trainers are immense.

What are the differences between outstanding trainers and the rest? There is now a practical answer to this question, provided by NLP modelling skills. They are published here for the first time and give you the knowledge and skill to learn faster, teach others to learn faster and improve the results you create.

- Discover how the skills of top trainers can work for you
- Communicate at different psychological levels simultaneously
- learn to improve your communication skills
- Enhance your self-confidence
- Turn difficult questions to your advantage
- Design and evaluate more effective training
- Increase your influence on training strategy

'A monumental feat the organisation of the fundamentals of training into a practical primer and valuable reference for anyone who wants to know more about designing effective ways to train.'

Christina Hall, M.A., The NLP Connection